# Weight
# TRAINING
## *for cyclists*

by *Ken Doyle* ATC, CSCS *and*
*Eric Schmitz* CSCS, HFI, CPT

**VELO**
*press*

BOULDER, COLORADO  USA

International Standard Book Number: 1-884737-43-9

Library of Congress Cataloging-in-Publication applied for.

**PRINTED IN THE USA**

VELO
*press*

1830 N. 55th Street • Boulder, Colorado • 80301-2700 • USA
303/440-0601 • FAX 303/444-6788 • E-MAIL velopress@7dogs.com

To purchase additional copies of this book or other Velo products, call 800/234-8356 or visit us on the Web at www.velocatalogue.com

# DISCLAIMER

The information and ideas in this book are for educational and instructional purposes and are not intended as prescriptive advice. Consult your physician before starting any exercise program, especially if you have been sedentary for several years, are over the age of 35, have a history of heart disease, or have any other medical condition that may require consultation before beginning a training program.

# ACKNOWLEDGMENTS

We would like to acknowledge Mark Saunders for his encouragement and dedication to getting this project going from the start. Thank you to Julie Main, the general manager at Santa Barbara Athletic Club, for letting us use the facility for our photographs, and our models—Mike Smith, Dave Lettieri, Kim Woodrum and Kristi Cooper for their outstanding athletic figures. Thanks to Robert Oliver for the great pictures, and Amy Sorrells at VeloPress for her understanding, guidance and patience.

*From Eric:* I would like to thank my wife, Ingrid, and daughter, Hanna, for putting up with the long hours of computer work and piles of research material. To my brother Mark, who is a constant entrepreneurial inspiration. Thanks to my sister, Rebecca, for always looking on the lighter side of life. My mother, MaryAnn, deserves a special acknowledgment for the inspiring parental support she has provided over the years.

*From Ken:* I would like to thank my parents, Mac and Judy, for always supporting me in my endeavors, be it athletic competitions or business ventures; they are always there for me. Thank you to Rebecca Kaye for her continued words of encouragement and support of Performance Enhancement Products; she's been a great help. Thank you to Perri, Marsha and Sharon who pushed me over the years to keep plugging away at my projects. My housemates Morgan and Kristin deserve mention for tolerating piles of research articles, journals and books spread evenly throughout the house for three months.

# TABLE OF CONTENTS

# PREFACE

*"The dictionary is the only place success comes before work. Hard work is the price we must all pay for success ..."*
*—Vince Lombardi*
*former NFL coach of the Green Bay Packers*

Do you have the type of character and dedication needed to progress beyond your current level of performance? Often the difference between success in life and one who falls just short of that is only a matter of a resilient character. It seems that everyone today is searching for low-effort ways to improve their lives, which is evidenced by the many fad diets, get-rich-quick schemes, and endless supplements and devices that promise incredible results. As the corny saying goes, "The good things in life take hard work and complete dedication to acquire."

In athletics, this is particularly true since most sports require a great deal of fitness and skill development to reach higher levels. If you are going to reach your full potential as a cyclist, you are going to have to rise to the challenge, and place forth the extra effort.

In addition to a resilient character, improvement in life comes to those who possess an open mind to new ideas. New forms of training as well as advances in technology are developed every year, and the most successful athletes and coaches adapt their programs accordingly. We hope that by incorporating the ideas introduced in this book, you will be able to raise the level of your performance to something you have only dreamed of in the past.

*Weight Training for Cyclists* was written to instruct and inspire you to participate in a year-round weight-training program. Designed with the cyclist specifically in mind, this book covers all that is essential to get you going or increase your knowledge if you already lift weights for training. The program that you will develop based on individual needs will have a direct and positive effect on your cycling performance.

After learning the basics and the rules that govern safe and effective weight training, we will teach you the specific form points of each individual exercise. Explosive strength development exercises will be added prior to the start of your racing season to give you the power needed to make winning moves on the bike. At the end of the book, there is a sample weight-training program that has been designed to bring you to your highest potential. With all of this information, you will formulate a program specifically to meet your training and performance needs.

We are pleased that you have taken the first step toward improved strength and performance by picking up this book. No matter what your background or performance goals are, *Weight Training for Cyclists* was written to support those efforts. Committing to a year-round weight-training program is a very important part of developing your full athletic potential.

Best of luck!

—*Ken Doyle and Eric Schmitz*

# CHAPTER ONE

# Weight Training
## *for a* Cyclist

---

*"When you train better, you become a better rider. You have to push yourself to the limit—that's what makes the top riders. Some people can't do it, but that's what makes the good ones and the great ones."*

—Sean Kelly
*Irish road racer, known as "the king of the classics"*

---

What would you do if a stranger told you that he had a guaranteed way of improving your speed, endurance and strength on a bike? Would you laugh in his face, or would you jump at the chance to become a better cyclist? If you laughed at him, then put this book down, continue to train as you always have, and receive the same results you have always received. If your answer was the latter, then read on, and learn how easy it is to incorporate weight training into your year-round cycling program. The benefits of a cycling-specific weight-training program will blow you away.

To reach your highest potential as a cyclist, you must go beyond simply piling on the training miles and hoping for the best. That kind of old-school thinking went out with wool jerseys. Today, competitive cyclists at all levels, both on- and off-road are using off-season and year-round weight training to improve their performance.

Forget all those antiquated myths about how weight lifting makes you bulky and awkward. We are not suggesting that you get pumped up like Arnold Schwarzenegger on two wheels. The truth is, optimum cycling performance demands total body strength. Cycling alone cannot completely develop the muscle groups used while riding. Most serious cyclists know that they should train with weights, but often they do not know the proper techniques or even where to start. If you don't have access to a qualified coach who understands the needs of competitive cyclists, then the information you've read in magazines and books on how to train might have proved so overwhelming that you never even got started. Following a program is easier than you might think, and gyms, for the most part, are no longer ruled by pumped-up meatheads. Visit a local gym and check it out, you'll see. Better yet, get a training partner and get started together.

It's a fact: Incorporating year-round cycling-specific weight training into your total training program will make you a better rider. The goal of this book is to simplify the most current scientific information on strength training, answer your questions about exercises and technique, and help you set up a year-round periodized training program specifically designed to enhance your cycling performance.

Did you know that weight training will not only improve your strength, but your endurance as well? In the past five years, there has been a wellspring of scientific research on the specifics of adding weight training to the training programs of endurance athletes. One of the ways in which weight training improves endurance is by increasing the time needed to reach total exhaustion at different levels of intensity. A stronger muscle uses a smaller amount of its total strength at a sub-maximal level, thus increasing the muscle's ability to work at that particular level. This could easily mean the difference be-tween hanging in, or getting dropped. Remember, the ability to push bigger gears for longer periods of time is what sepa-rates elite-level cyclists from the rest of the peloton.

By strengthening muscles that are specific to cycling, some studies have shown a 10- to 33-percent increase in endurance on a bike. When you consider that a vast number of criteriums, road races, cross-country mountain bike races and cyclo-cross races are won by inches, 10 to 30 percent could be the difference between standing on the podium and finishing with the pack. In theory, this improvement in endurance occurs because the in-creased strength of the slow-twitch (endurance) muscles allows them to do more work and spare the fast-twitch (sprinting) mus-cles for when you really need them. When you are forced to rely heavily on your fast-twitch muscles early in a race, you will burn up too much glycogen (stored blood sugar) and produce lactate. Soon after, you will be struggling just to hang onto the back of the pack. Wouldn't it be nice to be one of those riders that can keep a hard pace for the whole race, and then still hammer the final sprint!

If increased endurance isn't enough to get you to commit to weight training this off-season, then how about increased power? Everyone can use a better jump to answer attacks and initiate sprints. That kind of explosive activity requires a specific progression of exercises designed to increase the power you can apply to the pedals when it's show time. In addition, by increasing your power-to-weight ratio, you will sprint faster and longer, and climb better. Now we know that this is an area that everyone would like to improve on! Developing that strength simply by riding is not nearly as effective. In the gym, you can train the muscles to be more explosive, and then carry that power over to the bike when you begin specific on-the-bike drills during the pre-season.

Obviously, weight training alone will not make you a better cyclist. In combination with a periodized on-the-bike training program, weight training can give you a solid strength base to carry over to the bike, helping you to move closer to your full potential. Weight training can also balance out the strength ratios of your legs, giving you a more efficient pedal stroke, and help to prevent injuries.

We all understand the importance of developing leg strength for cycling, but you must not neglect the rest of your muscle groups. It is very important for the cyclist to have a strong lower back, which allows you to stay in a more aerodynamic position for longer periods of time without discomfort. Upper body strength gives you more control in a sprint or on an out-of-the-saddle climb. In cross-country and downhill mountain-bike races, in which maneuvering, climbing and control are essential to success, upper body strength is an absolute must. Overall body strength also helps increase stability on the bike, which aids in the power transfer to the pedals.

[ A STRONG BODY IS BETTER ABLE TO SURVIVE A CRASH ]

A stronger, strength-trained athlete will fair far better in the event of a crash, recover faster from injury, and reduce the risk of many "overuse" injuries.

Even with all these reasons to strength train, many cyclists are still reluctant to add weight training to their annual training program. Many fear gaining weight. Others protest that they don't have time. Some just loath spending time indoors. And then, there is the silent majority of cyclists who just don't know how to get started. The list goes on, and there are probably as many different excuses as there are cyclists. All of the myths about weight training adding too much bulk and eating up your training time are simply not true. Modern weight-lifting programs are scientific in their design and very time efficient. You won't end up looking like a body builder or spending all your free time in the gym.

[ VICTORY! ]

# CHAPTER TWO

# *The* Basics
# *of* Weight
# Training

---

*"The method is the same for you as it is for the pros.*
*What is different is the work load."*
— *Michele Ferrari*
*pro cycling coach*

I n this chapter, we will discuss the basics of weight training so that we may answer most of the questions that arise when starting a new program. This book is written for people with all levels of weight training experience from rookie to pro. Even if you have been lifting for years and years, it won't hurt to review the basics, chances are very good that you still have a few things to learn.

## CHOOSING A FACILITY

N ow that you've made the commitment to utilize weight training to improve cycling, you need to decide where to work out. If there is not a functional gym in your home, then you will have to make a decision as to which type of facility you would like to train. There are basically three types to choose from:

- Health clubs and spas
- Bodybuilding gyms
- School gyms and recreation centers

## PUBLIC GYMS

Check out the different gyms in your area to see if they meet your needs. Many facilities will allow you a free trial work-out if you tell them you may be interested in joining. If possible, visit the gym at the time that you will usually be training—this will allow you to observe the clientele who will be sharing the facility with you, as well as check on over-crowding. Here is a list of considerations:

- Is it in a convenient location? A facility close to home or work is preferable.
- Is the facility clean and well laid out?
- Does it have a knowledgeable, educated staff? (See *How to Choose a Trainer* in the next section).
- Does it have the appropriate equipment for your pro-grammed exercises?
- Check the condition of the machines. Are they dirty or in need of repair?
- What are the hours of operation? Does it work with your schedule?
- Does the facility offer shower and locker facilities? This can be very important if you train before work or during lunch time.
- And oh yes, what is the initial cost to join, and the monthly dues? Ask if there are any specials being offered?

Many facilities offer a non-prime-time discount membership rate for those who will not be training during peak hours.

## HOME GYMS

A home gym holds certain advantages over a public gym. Exercising at home is convenient, and there are no crowds to contend with. You will save a lot of time by not having to drive to and from a facility, which can be a big plus in severe weather. And, in the long run, it may be more economical to invest in the equipment required to outfit a home facility, than it would be to pay initiation fees and monthly dues at a public gym.

Of course, the home gym does have its disadvantages, as well. Equipment limitations may keep you from performing some key exercises. Since some people respond better in an environment in which they can feed off of the energy of the people surrounding them, motivation may prove to be more difficult if you exercise alone. Likewise, there may be more distractions at home than in a large facility. Whatever your preference, consider finding a workout partner. Having someone else to train with can be one of the greatest motivators there is.

To set up a home gym, you will need the proper equipment and space—preferably a well-lit, well-ventilated area that measures at least 10 ft. by 10 ft. Here is a list of the basic equipment needed to set up a functional home gym:
  • A sturdy, flat bench
  • An adjustable barbell set
  • An adjustable dumbbell set

With these three items, you will be able to perform many of the different exercises in the program. And, with the addition of a pair of squat standards, you will be able to safely perform the squat, which is a core exercise of the cyclist's weight-training program.

The most difficult exercise to perform in a home setting is the leg curl, which works the hamstrings. This is a very important muscle group for cyclists to develop, one which cannot be safely and efficiently exercised without a proper leg-curl machine or bench attachment. Many of the lower-priced devices on the market are not adjustable to different leg lengths, and may put the athlete into an unsafe resistance arc while performing the exercise.

## TYPES OF EQUIPMENT

Today, there are a lot of different types of resistance exercise equipment on the market. Hundreds of companies are producing machines, equipment, and various devices for the purpose of exercise. It may take a little bit of experimenting to find out what type works best for you.

### FREE WEIGHTS

Free weights make up the most basic workout equipment in resistance training, consisting of barbells and dumbbells. They epitomize the essence of weight training, dating back to the athletes of ancient Greece.

Barbell exercises are performed using a 7-feet-long Olympic barbell bar—which weighs 45 pounds. unloaded—and different-sized weight plates ranging from 2-$^1/_2$ to 45 pounds. However, many facilities also feature a rack of fixed-weight barbells

[   OLYMPIC BARBELL AND WEIGHTS   ]

[   FIXED DUMBBELLS
ON THE RACK   ]

11

generally ranging from 10 to 150 pounds each. Most home gyms utilize a lighter weight, standard 6-foot-bar and weight-plate set.

Dumbbells, basically, are a shorter version of the barbell, and are designed to be held by one hand. In most public gyms you will find sets of fixed dumbbells available in a large range of weights. In home gyms, adjustable dumbbell sets are the most commonly used, but it can be very convenient to own fixed-weight dumbbells in the weights you will most likely use.

***Pros of free weights*** Exercises may be performed in a very functional manner. Dumbbells may be used to imitate motions found in sport or daily activities; free weights require greater coordination and balance to perform than other modes of resistance training, which leads to increased joint stabilization.

***Cons of free weights*** When using free weights, you are working against gravity. Thus, it may be very difficult to work specific muscle groups as effectively as it would be on a resistance machine that is built specifically for that purpose. Also, free-weight exercises may be difficult for beginners, and can lead to injury if not performed correctly.

## ACCESSORY EQUIPMENT

To perform many free-weight exercises, it is necessary to use special benches—flat, incline, decline and upright—to safely position yourself to perform specific exercises efficiently. Also, assorted weight bars and cable handle attachments may be used to work specific muscle groups. To store loose equipment and assist you in certain exercises, special racks are available in most facilities.

[ A FULLY ADJUSTABLE BENCH ]

## RESISTANCE MACHINES

There is a tremendous variety of resistance weight-training machines on the market today. The most common type found in clubs and gyms utilize a weight stack connected to a lever bar by chains and cables. The weights can be changed easily by changing the pin placement in the stack.

The first machines built for gym use were designed by Harold Zinkin in the 1950s. Soon, Zinkin's Universal Gym machines were found in nearly every gym from high schools to health clubs. These machines were commonly multistationed, allowing an entire group to use them at one time to perform a large variety of exercises. The Universal Gym greatly simplified weight training, making it more appealing, especially to newcomers.

The next stage in resistance weight-training machines

[ EXAMPLE OF AN OFF-CENTER CAM ]

came in the 1960s with the development of Nautilus machines by Arthur Jones. These machines utilized an off-center cam designed to provide a perfectly balanced resistance throughout the full range of motion of the exercise.

By the 1970s, Nautilus machines were found in gyms and clubs nationwide. Their popularity continued to grow, and even today they can be found in facilities around the world.

The 1980s saw dozens of companies jumping into the resistance-machine market. Suddenly, there were many machines that closely resembled the Universal and Nautilus predecessors. Competition brought about new innovations in machine development.

One of the complaints of earlier models was that they did not properly fit different-sized people. Another complaint was that there were no range-of-motion adjustments. Weight machine manufacturers answered these issues by designing equipment with more and more special features. Most machines can now be set to a special fit for each user, which is a special plus for people with orthopedic limitations and rehabilitation applications.

Throughout the years, there has also been a boom in resistance weight machines for the home market. To this day, the market for home exercise equipment remains very strong. While the quality and design of some machines is suspect, there are many very good pieces of equipment available that are close to commercial gym quality, however, you must be willing to pay for it.

[ RANGE OF MOTION ADJUSTABILITY ON THE CAM ]

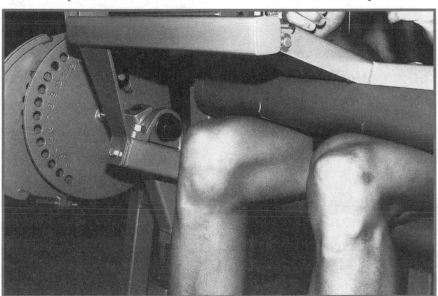

*Pros of resistance weight machines*   Machines are safer and easier to use than free weights. They allow for specific, isolated movements that are either difficult or impossible to perform with free weights. The weights can also be changed quickly, allowing for a speedier workout. And finally, resistance can be provided over a full range of motion for each muscle group.

*Cons of resistance weight machines*   By limiting the user to single-joint movements in fixed planes of motion, machines do not promote the balance, coordination and joint stabilization that comes from using free weights. Weight machines are also very expensive and take up a lot of space. And the range-of-motion adjustments that are available with some machines may not fit the user properly.

### RESISTANCE BANDS

A simple and inexpensive technique of applying resistance to the muscles is with the use of elastic resistance bands. Once an exercise mode limited to physical therapy rehabilitation using surgical tubing, resistance bands are now found at nearly all workout facilities. Now, there are a variety of resistance band products available on the market. The ease and safety of use makes them perfect for those just getting started in strength training. Resis-

[ STRENGTHENING THE SHOULDER WITH A RESISTANCE BAND ]

tance bands are very effective for isolating specific, small muscle groups as well as performing complex multiplane exercises that simulate sports motions. While there are many exercises that may be performed using resistance bands, their use is limited to warm-ups, light strengthening and rehabilitation. Some large muscle groups may be difficult to work effectively using this resistance method.

## PERSONAL EQUIPMENT AND CLOTHING

**CLOTHING**  It may seem silly to have to be told what to wear to the gym, but you would be surprised what some people show up in. The most important thing is to wear something comfortable that allows full movement, and isn't too hot. Gone are the days when the amount of sweat was the measure of a good workout.

**GLOVES**  Weight lifting gloves are designed to prevent hands from slipping off the bars or grips. They have padded palms and cut off fingertips, much like bike gloves. Most bike gloves have too much padding for a good barbell grip, but may be useful in a pinch.

**SHOES**  It is very important that the shoes worn while lifting weights are very supportive and cushioned. Do not wear running shoes, loose-fitting shoes, or thongs because you could slip or lose some toes, then those new $200 bike shoes won't quite fit. Mishaps happen when least expected; protect yourself.

**WEIGHT BELTS**  Weightlifting belts are highly recommended, especially when performing heavy or high-risk exercises, such as squats, power cleans and deadlifts. Weight belts come in different widths, waist sizes and materials—nylon or leather. Many people favor the newer nylon belts because they don't require a breaking-in period, while most diehards prefer leather.

## HOW TO CHOOSE A TRAINER OR A COACH

Ideally, we would all have a qualified coach to design and implement a program for us. He or she would oversee all of our workouts, making sure that we warm up and stretch, that our exercise form is correct, and that proper rest intervals are taken between sets—and they would keep us motivated to work toward our goals. Unfortunately, we do not all have coaches to help us through each workout. If we all did, there would be no reason to read this book.

Even though the main purpose of this book is to inform

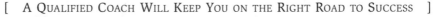

[ A QUALIFIED COACH WILL KEEP YOU ON THE RIGHT ROAD TO SUCCESS ]

cyclists on the proper way to design year-round weight-training programs, and the correct way to perform each exercise, we highly encourage you to seek out the advice of a qualified fitness trainer, even if just for an hour twice per year. One-on-one instruction can be very motivating and beneficial, especially in the early stages of weight training. It is very important that the person you choose to work with has high qualifications. Otherwise, the information you are getting may not help, and, actually, may hurt you.

## QUALITIES TO LOOK FOR

**K**eep this in mind while shopping around for a trainer to help you: The term *certified trainer* tells nothing about a person's qualifications. There are currently numerous certifications offered by different organizations. Some of these organizations are well-established and hold very high testing standards before certifying a trainer. Some require a college degree from applicants, while others have no education requirement whatsoever. The field of personal training is one of the fastest growing in the nation. It seems that every man or woman who ever lifted a weight—and many who have not—are jumping on the bandwagon to make big bucks in the fitness business. As a consumer, you need to make an informed decision when choosing a trainer. Protect yourself by asking a potential training coach the following questions:

• Are you certified? If so, by what organization(s)?

Look for one or more of these: the National Strength and Conditioning Association (NSCA); American College of Sports Medicine (ACSM); or the National Academy of Sports Medicine (NASM).

- Do you have a college education? What did you major in? Is it a science or exercise-related degree?
- What is your experience as a trainer? Other background?
- What is your training philosophy?
- Are you familiar with the training needs of a cyclist? Ask him or her what those are, and see if they match up with the concepts and program found in this book. A good trainer will be open to having you share your program, then work on it with you.
- May I call any of your other clients for a referral?
- What is the fee per session? Is there a discount for buying five or more sessions in advance?

Whether you will be hiring a trainer just to introduce you to the equipment and check your form, or will be meeting with him or her for every training session you do, you need to make sure that your personalities mesh. This may be difficult to judge in your first introduction, but if you feel that your trainer is not motivating, or does not possess good teaching skills, move on to another. Remember, you are the consumer and athlete, and you deserve to work with the best person available.

## GYM ETIQUETTE

The gym is another world. There is a complete subculture of people there who, hopefully, live by a special set of unwritten rules of conduct. Most things are common sense, but there are a few rituals you might need to become aware of. The following is a quick run-down of these common courtesies, and we've placed them in order of our pet peeves.

## RERACK YOUR WEIGHTS

This is as simple as mom used to put it, "Put your toys away when you're finished playing with them!"

There are two subcategories here:

**1)** Putting dumbbells and barbells back in the proper place when you are finished with them.

**2)** Stripping the weight plates off of a bar or machine when you are done using it, even if it wasn't empty when you got to it.

Nothing can trash a gym faster than misplaced equipment.

[ A WEIGHT TREE
USED TO STORE
BARBELL PLATES ]

Help keep the weight room safe and functional by reracking, and encouraging others to do the same.

## EXERCISE WITH A TOWEL

Place a towel down on the cushion when using a machine, and be certain to wipe up any sweat you may have left on the grips. You don't want to lie in someone else's pool of perspiration, and vice-versa.

## SHARE THE EQUIPMENT

In a crowded gym, such as at 5:00 p.m., there are a lot of people trying to use the same equipment. If you see someone resting at a machine between sets, simply ask, "Can I work in with you?" Most often the person will get up and let you use the machine while they rest. Remember, if you change the adjustments on the machine, return them to how you found them after your set.

## ACQUIRE SPATIAL AWARENESS

Especially in free-weight situations, there is a lot of opportunity to move about the room to perform exercises. If you are standing, or have moved a bench to use, be aware that you are not blocking traffic or interfering with someone else's exercise. And do not stand between someone and the mirror when they are using it.

## WATCH THE NOISE

Different facilities, obviously, have different acceptable noise levels. Some places cater to hard-core bodybuilders and power lifters, and crank up heavy metal music to a deafening level. Other places cater to families or a more mature crowd, and choose to play Muzak. Whatever the case, be aware of the noise you are making, be it excessive grunting and groaning, or loose headphones that let the whole room share in your secret motivational tunes.

## USE THE LOCKERS

Some gyms resemble a twelve-year-old's room: gym bags, sweatshirts, water bottles, towels and books litter every corner. Keep your stuff stowed away from the workout area.

## SAFETY

We cannot emphasize enough how important it is to learn and follow the rules of safety, especially when training in a public facility. As is the case in most instances, common sense is the first step toward increasing safety. In the next chapter you will notice that safety is the first of our 10 rules of weight training.

## GENERAL NUTRITION

Sad as it is, many, and maybe even *most* athletes are undereducated on the importance of proper nutrition, and the critical part it can play in performances. Eating a proper diet will improve overall performance both on and off of the bike by helping to reduce body fat, fuel the body for hard training, improve recovery after training, and become a healthier person in general.

## THE SKINNY ON FAT

During the "carbohydrate craze" of the early 1980s, fat was officially labeled the athlete's enemy. Everyone was obsessed with severely limiting, or eliminating, fat from their diets altogether. It was a pasta-and-bagel world, with athletes bragging to each other about how high they had made the carbohydrate percentage of their diets. What was being overlooked was the fact that there were certain essential fats that the body needed to remain healthy. Not *all* fats are bad for you. Monosaturated and omega-3 fats are the good ones; saturated fats are the bad ones. Try to stay clear of saturated and partially hydrogenated fats, and keep your overall intake of fat to less than 30 percent of total caloric intake.

## WHAT ABOUT PROTEIN?

For many years, a high-protein diet has been associated with weight lifting and bodybuilding. Visions of big meatheads gulping down raw eggs and eating Fred Flintstone steaks come to most people's minds when asked about the protein needs of athletes. The truth is, the protein demands of athletes are not much higher than that of the average person. Currently, the Recommended Dietary Allowance (RDA) of protein is 0.8 grams per kilogram of body weight. The increased protein needs of a weight-training athlete would be between 1 and 1.5 grams per kilogram. This may seem like a significant increase except for the fact that most Americans are already eating twice the recommended amount of protein, anyway. The best advice is to emphasize slightly more protein in the diet that come from low-fat sources.

## WE STILL LOVE CARBS

As previously mentioned, there has been a "carbohydrate craze" among athletes since the 1980s, and it still lives on in the minds of many people. First of all, there is nothing wrong with athletes consuming a lot of carbohydrates. Carbohydrates are the primary fuel used in muscular contractions. The energy released from carbohydrates can be released within exercising muscles up to three times faster than energy from fat. Some carbohydrates enter the bloodstream quickly and give an immediate energy boost, but this dramatic rise can also lead to a dramatic fall. By combining carbohydrates with protein-rich low-fat foods, you're energy level will tend to remain steady, and your appetite will stay satisfied longer.

## MORE TIPS ON NUTRITION:

**GRAZING**   Eat several smaller meals throughout the day rather than the typical big three. This will help keep blood sugar levels more constant, as well as control your appetite.

**EAT AFTER YOU WORK OUT**   Carbohydrate (glycogen) stores in the body are limited. You must replenish these depleted stores following a hard work-out. Most cyclists are good about this following a hard ride, but the same holds true after a vigorous weight-training session. Within 30 minutes of the completion of your work-out, the body is much more capable of replenishing the fuel stores that you just used. During this "window" of time, try to consume carbohydrates and protein in the form of a snack, small meal, or even a recovery sports drink. You will perform far better tomorrow.

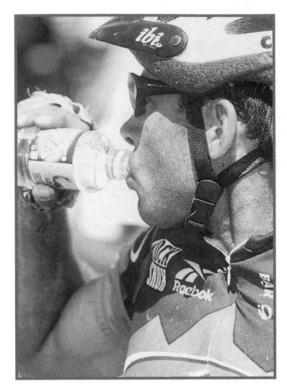

[ HYDRATION BEGINS
LONG BEFORE YOU ARE
ON THE BIKE ]

**BE A CAMEL**  You would be hard-pressed to drink too much water in a day. In fact, most athletes fall well short in the hydration department. Dehydration may be the most common cause of premature fatigue during sports training and competition. Even low levels of dehydration impair physiological function and hurt performance. You need to drink eight to twelve 8-ounce glasses (2-3 liters) of water per day. And if the weather is hot, or you have been training harder than usual, that amount needs to be increased. If you are well-hydrated, you should be urinating a clear stream about every two hours.

## A FEW WORDS ON SUPPLEMENTS

There are a tremendous number of dietary or "nutritional" supplements available on the market today. While it is not within the scope of this book to address each one individually, we will offer the following:

By definition, a supplement is something added to the diet to make up for a deficiency. If you suffer from a nutritional deficiency, then supplementation may be indicated for you. If you are seeking out a miracle supplement to increase your muscle development, drop body fat, stimulate your energy level, strength or endurance, then you are just the person that the manufacturers are aiming at. The old saying, "If something sounds too good to be true, it probably is," is true of most dietary supplements that are out there.

We've all seen the magazine ads, especially those in muscle magazines. They all look good—really good. The claims they make are incredible, and to many, very inviting. The manufacturers, distributors and retailers of supplements rely mainly on such advertising to market their goods. Have you ever noticed that these companies do not make the same unsupported claims on the product label? In fact, if there is anything at all on the label, it is usually a disclaimer stating that the effect of the supplement has not been evaluated by the Food and Drug Administration.

Therefore, if the supplement does not claim to do anything, then it is probably just a food product. One thing each one of these products *is* guaranteed to do—whether it works or not—is make you a little lighter ... in the wallet. This is not to say that there aren't some supplements out there that may improve performance. But if you *do* want to add supplements to your program, please heed the following advice.

## What you should do

First of all, do not get your nutritional advice from advertisements or meatheads in the gym. If you can, set up an appointment with a registered dietitian to get your questions answered. If you cannot do that, then at least investigate product advertisements which may be biased and deceiving. Look for the following warning signs:

• The product claims are not backed up with scientific research.

• If there is research introduced, has it been presented in a scientific journal?

• Check to see if the manufacturer conducted the research themselves.

• Does the manufacturer own or publish the journal in which the research was presented?

• Are the research findings taken out of context with the claims?

• Is the supplement promoted by sponsored, high-profile athletes or celebrities?

Most times there is no credible basis for the claims made of supplements by the manufacturers. Not only may some products provide no claimed effect, they may be downright dangerous for you to use. Use good judgment as a consumer, and realize that there is no substitute for proper nutrition. In fact, it has been stated in research that "there are no known nutritional deficiencies associated with sport training that would necessitate supplementation over normal ingestion of food and drink." More times than not, our advice to athletes is to take the amount of money they were about to spend on a miracle supplement, and spend it at a good produce market.

## BEFORE YOU START

It is very important to ***warm up*** and ***stretch*** prior to a weight-lifting workout. Time may be short, and there may be temptation to skip this part of the program. Don't do it! In doing so, you will be greatly increasing your risk of injury and decreased performance.

## WARM UP

The purpose of the warm-up is to increase deep muscle temperature by increasing blood flow. Muscles that are warm have a greater amount of flexibility that reduces the risk of injury.

The warm-up is about a 10- to 15-minute session of gentle

aerobic activity, just enough to break into a light sweat. This could be in the form of jogging, stationary cycling, stairclimbing, or by using another piece of cardiovascular equipment.

## STRETCHING

Flexibility is a very important component of fitness, and possibly the most overlooked by both athletes and coaches. Performing a good stretching routine on a regular basis is key to increasing

[ TAKE THE TIME TO WARM UP
BEFORE LIFTING ]

flexibility, joint efficiency, and decreasing the risk of injuries. Former Motorola team physician Dr. Massimo Testa sites a study that has shown how cyclists may increase their power by 5 percent by merely stretching the hamstrings; the added flexibility leads to better utilization of the quadriceps. If hamstrings are tight, they will work *against* the quads during the downstroke, preventing the leg from straightening efficiently. A joint that can easily move through its full range of motion will allow for greater application of force throughout that range of motion.

Cyclists tend to lose flexibility in the leg muscles because the activity of pedaling a bike does not require full range of motion. In addition, the muscles of the lower back and neck can tighten as a result of holding a riding position for many hours. While it is important to target these areas for stretching, a general overall flexibility program must be followed, one which includes all of the joints of the body. This may sound like a tremendous undertaking in an already tight work-out schedule, but the truth is an effective total body flexibility program can be performed in about 15 minutes.

## TIPS ON STRETCHING

**DO NOT STRETCH COLD MUSCLES** Do a light warm-up if you are going to stretch before your work-out. Pre-work-out stretching should be kept simple and short, with the serious flexibility program being performed *after* a bike ride or weight-training work-out.

**DON'T FORCE IT** Stretch to the point where you feel mild tension, then relax and hold each stretch for ten to thirty seconds without bouncing. A stretch should not cause pain or discomfort.

**BREATHE, BREATHE, BREATHE** Do not hold your breath while stretching. If you do, you are probably trying too hard. Breathe deeply and naturally while holding each stretch.

**BE CONSISTENT** Daily stretching is the best program, but benefits can be had from stretching at least three days a week. We strongly encourage you to get in the habit of stretching following hard work-outs. It is a good way to cool down, and it helps to reduce muscle soreness the next day.

## DIFFERENT STRETCHING TECHNIQUES

**TRADITIONAL STATIC** This technique of stretching is the one that most people are familiar with. Traditional stretching incorporates all of the above tips while the athlete positions him or herself in a specific position to emphasize flexibility in a chosen muscle and joint. The body is held still—static—and the stretch is performed by keeping the muscle relaxed while gently increasing range of motion.

**ASSISTED STATIC** This is basically the same as traditional static stretching except that a partner is used to assist the athlete in gaining range of motion. With this technique, the partner helps hold the position and gently pushes or pulls you to more of a stretch than you may be able to perform alone. One of the big benefits of this technique is that, generally, it is easier to relax and get an efficient stretch with the light pressure assistance of a partner. Good communication is very important to prevent over stretching and injury.

**ACTIVE ISOLATED (AI)** This stretching technique has become much more popular in recent years. Active Isolated stretching utilizes short duration stretches —two seconds—of a

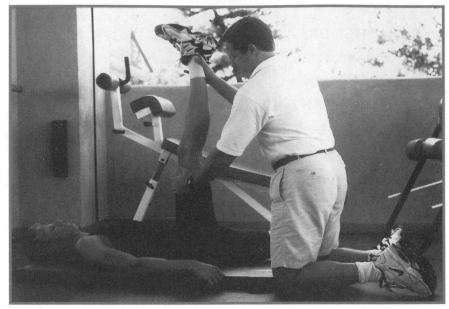

[ ASSISTED STATIC STRETCH ]

[ ACTIVE ISOLATED STRETCH ]

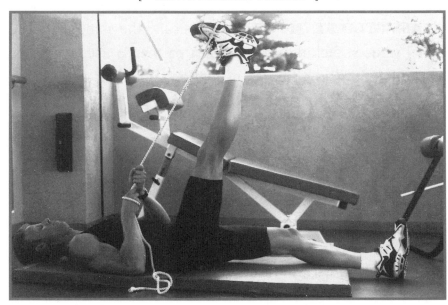

target muscle immediately following the tightening of the muscle located opposite it. This process is repeated eight to twelve times. The theory behind this technique is that the stretch reflex of the muscle—which is the natural response of a muscle to shorten when overstretched—will not be activated with such a short effort. AI stretches are very specific and not as easy to perform as traditional stretches. Most require some practice and strict attention to proper technique.

**PROPRIOCEPTIVE NEUROMUSCULAR FACILITA-TION (PNF)** This technique is similar to Active Isolated stretching in that it involves a muscular contraction prior to the stretch phase. The difference with PNF stretching, is that the muscle intended for stretching is tightened for about five seconds, then it is relaxed and static-stretched for another five seconds, repeating three to five times. Some PNF stretches are

[ PNF ]

better performed by using a partner to assist in the stretch. The theory is that the muscle overrides the stretch reflex contraction and then becomes less resistant to the stretching.

## TEN BASIC PRE-LIFTING STRETCHES

**N**ow that you know all about the importance of stretching prior to lifting weights, we are going to show you ten basic static stretches that will cover the bases prior to pumping iron. Keep in mind that this is a very basic program. You may prefer to add stretches that utilize one or more of the techniques other than static to your program. Additionally, we encourage you to add more stretches, especially for the hamstrings, and any other super tight muscle groups.

### BASIC STRETCHING ROUTINE

**Perform each exercise three to five times**

### 1. SHOULDER-CHEST STRETCH

While standing, clasp your hands with fingers interlaced behind your back. Slowly straighten your arms and lift them upward until you feel a mild stretch in the chest area. Hold stretched position 15-30 seconds.

## 2. POSTERIOR SHOULDER STRETCH

While standing, place one arm across body. Gently pull the arm with the other hand grabbing above the elbow. Hold for 15-30 seconds and repeat with the other arm.

## 3. TRICEPS STRETCH

Grasp a rolled towel behind your head with one arm coming from the top and one from the bottom. Gently pull downward on the towel to stretch the muscle. Point the top elbow toward the ceiling and hold the stretch for 15-30 seconds.

## 4. QUADRICEPS STRETCH

While standing, reach behind and gently pull your foot close to your gluteal muscles, pointing knee downward. Hold on to a wall or table for extra support. Maintain the position for 15-30 seconds, and repeat with other leg.

## 5. CAT AND CAMEL STRETCH

Start on all fours and slowly round the back by contracting the abdominal muscles. Look between your knees, feeling the muscles stretch along your spine. Alternate that position with one of arching your back downward, stretching your abdominal region. Repeat 10 times holding each position for about 5-10 seconds.

## 6. GROIN STRETCH

Starting in a seated position, bring the soles of your feet together, facing each other. While holding them above the ankle joint, gently push on the inside of the thighs, feeling the stretch in your inner thigh area. Hold that position for 15-30 seconds. To increase the stretch, slowly bend forward from the waist keeping the back straight.

## 7. HAMSTRING-CALF STRETCH

From the groin stretch position slowly straighten one leg keeping the toe pointing toward the ceiling. With your leg in front of you, bend forward from the waist keeping your back straight. To increase the stretch in the calf area, slowly move the toe toward your hips. Hold the forward position of the stretch for 15-30 seconds and repeat on the other side.

## 8. FIGURE 4-GLUTEAL STRETCH

Lie on your back and bring both knees towards your chest. Cross one leg over the other to form the number four. Grab the leg that remains perpendicular to the floor above the knee, and gently pull toward your head. Hold the stretch for 15-30 seconds and repeat on the other side.

### 9. KNEE TO CHEST STRETCH

From a position of lying on your back bring one knee toward your chest, and grasp it just below the knee. Gently pull the leg toward your chest, feeling the tension release in the low back area. Be careful not to pull too hard on the knee. Hold the position of stretch for 15-30 seconds, then switch legs.

### 10. PRESS-UP

Start by lying on your stomach with your hands under your shoulders. Slowly press up with your arms, keeping your hips on the floor. Stretch for a position of straight arms while your hips remain on the floor. Hold the top position for 15-30 seconds.

### YOU'RE READY FOR THE NEXT STEP!

Now you know the basic information you'll need to get started. The next chapter will take you one step closer by explaining more specifically the concepts of weight training, and considerations taken when designing a personal program.

# CHAPTER THREE

# Fundamental
## Rules of Weight
# Training

*"The difference between failure and success is doing a thing nearly right and doing it exactly right."*
—Edward Simmons
American painter

To get the best results from most things in life you need to play "by the rules." If one or more of the rules are violated, you will have to pay the price by achieving a lesser result. Paying the price for not following the rules in weight training means risking being over trained, over tired, or possibly injured. Remember, you are participating in a strength training program to get stronger and to improve your performance on the bike, not to be the next Mr. or Miss Universe. Train smart, and follow the rules explained in this book.

The rules center on safety and how to achieve optimum results from resistance training. For example, it is very hard to improve your performance in the off-season if you jump into squatting exercises right away without taking the time to learn the proper technique, then, consequently, blow out your knee from going down too far. It is no coincidence that the first rule in this chapter covers safety issues. We cannot emphasize enough, the importance of being safe in the weight room. This chapter will teach you the basic rules you need to know in order for your weight-training program to be a success. Take the time to read and learn it thoroughly.

## RULE NO. 1
## ALWAYS PAY ATTENTION TO SAFETY!

### PREPARE YOUR BODY TO LIFT

We recommend a three-part warm-up procedure to get the most out of your strength training work-outs. The first and second parts of the warm-up were covered in the previous chapter, and consist of the light aerobic exercise session followed by a stretching program. As we stated earlier, do not be tempted to skip stretching because you are short of time or anxious to get started. If you make proper preparation a habit from the start, then it will be a natural part of your weight-training program every time you go into the gym.

Part three of the warm-up actually occurs throughout the entire strength training session. Performing a warm-up set for every exercise allows you to get ready for that particular lift, both mentally and physically. Pick a weight that is 50 percent of the weight that you will use in your first working set and perform about 15 to 20 repititions. Shift your focus to the exercise at hand, concentrating on the muscle groups that will be utilized, and the proper form of the lift. Once this set is completed, your muscles will be ready for the working sets, and a solid muscle motor pattern will have been established.

## LIFT SLOWLY DURING BASE STRENGTH BUILDING

Most of the exercises you will be executing to obtain your base of strength should be performed in a slow and controlled manner. Weight lifting is performed in this way to protect the soft tissue surrounding the joint. This soft tissue automatically absorbs the inertia created by a change in direction of a weight moving too fast, and can be damaged. In order to reduce the risk of injury, lift at a pace equal to two counts during the concentric (lifting) phase, hold for a count of one at peak contraction, and lower for two to four counts during the eccentric (lowering) phase. The only exceptions are the more advanced, specialized power development exercises: cleans and plyometrics. These power exercises, covered in Chapter 7, will be incorporated into your program only after you have developed a solid strength base from the isotonic lifts.

## DON'T BE A BLOWFISH

Improper breathing during lifting can be hazardous. If you close off your throat during exhalation and hold your breath, a phenomenon called the Valsalva maneuver is created. This event can be dangerous due to the fact that it dramatically raises your systolic blood pressure. This strong rise in blood pressure can aggravate any weakness you might have in your cardiovascular system. In addition to the rapid rise in blood pressure, the Valsalva maneuver can also limit the blood supply to the brain. This limited blood supply frequently causes dizziness and possible fainting.

To avoid any of these problems, get in the habit of breathing in the rhythmic pattern of exhaling on the concentric—muscle shortening—phase of the lift, and inhaling during the eccentric—muscle lengthening—phase. If you have trouble remembering when to inhale and when to exhale, just remember that you are trying to blow the weight up. If the weight is going up, the air is going out.

Another thing to note about breathing during lifting is that it is possible to "over breathe." This happens quite often when someone blows off too much air, causing hyperventilation. If dizziness occurs while breathing, you are probably hyperventilating. A quick remedy to bring carbon dioxide levels back up and control hyperventilation is to exhale and then hold your breath for a few seconds. Of course, you will not perform this procedure during a lift. By exhaling then holding the breath, the problem should be quickly relieved.

## PROPER REST, PERFECT RESULTS

A safety issue that is often overlooked is taking adequate rest intervals. Trying to work-out when you haven't recovered enough between sets or between work-outs is inviting the risk of serious injury and second-rate results. Performing complex, high-intensity lifts when fatigued, such as power cleans, is very dangerous and should never be attempted. Make sure to follow the guidelines on rest intervals between sets and work-outs covered in Chapters 8 and 9.

## WEIGHT MACHINE SAFETY TIPS

Utilizing weight machines—stack, plate loaded, or specialized types such as air, water and computerized—during your work-outs is a great way to bring comprehensive muscle isolation to your weakest areas. Taking note of the following pointers will aid you in injury-free machine work-outs:

**1. MAKE SURE THE MACHINE IS ADJUSTED PROPERLY.** This is extremely important in order to insure safety. The easiest way to remember this is to be sure the joint you are working lines up with the axis of rotation on the machine. The joint's axis of rotation is the central spot in the exercise in which movement takes place, such as the elbow in a biceps curl, or the knee in a hamstring curl.

**2. PERFORM THE EXERCISE WITH THE PROPER SPEED.** Momentum may allow you to lift more weight and impress others, but it will also rob you of some potential strength development. Remember, soft tissue will take on an unwanted strain if you are lifting fast and jerky. Don't risk it.

**3. MAKE SURE THAT THE MACHINE YOU ARE GOING TO USE IS FUNCTIONING PROPERLY.** This may sound silly, but we have seen many people try to use machines that clearly weren't working properly. Use common sense in machine selection. Look, listen and feel what is going on while on the machine. Make sure to report any problems to the fitness staff right away. Hopefully, they will appreciate it. We recommend only working out at a facility that carries complete maintenance records on all their machines, and promptly fixes broken equipment.

**4. USE THE MACHINE AS IT WAS INTENDED TO BE USED.**
Follow the instructions given by the manufacturer, and do not try
new ways to utilize the machine. There are plenty of fools out
there inventing exercises of their own. Do not be influenced by
them. If you are, you are only inviting injury due to improper use.
If you have questions, ask a qualified trainer for help.

**5. FOLLOW THE PRINCIPLES OF PROPER RESISTANCE
PROGRAMMING.** Don't go gangbusters and change everything you've been doing simply because the gym got the lat-
est and greatest machines. Stick with your training program,
and learn to incorporate the new machines into it. Your training program is set up to achieve short- and long-term goals.
You must be consistent with them in order to be successful.

### FREE WEIGHT SAFETY TIPS

The unstable nature of free-weight exercises is necessary
to improve the strength and joint stability required for cycling,
but adds to the risk of injury during your workout. Follow the
steps below to reduce the chance of lost training time:

**1. WHEN LOADING A BAR TO PERFORM A FREE-
WEIGHT EXERCISE, USE COMMON SENSE.** Carefully move
the weight plates from the weight tree to the bar using proper
form. Do not lift a heavy weight plate with just one arm. Lifting
with one arm puts an unequal rotational load on the lower back
and shoulders, inviting injury. Instead, lift with both hands plac-
ing the weight plate parallel to your shoulders. Your spine
should stay in a neutral position during the movement. Do not
bend forward at the waist while holding a heavy plate. Instead,
be sure to bend at the knees and keep your chin up.

[ PROPER FORM ]

**2. USE COLLARS.** If you do not use collars, you are seriously impacting your level of safety. If you have ever been in a gym when a plate falls off, sending the bar flying in the opposite direction, then you are already sold on the need for collars. It only takes a second to slap them on, so do it.

[ SAFETY COLLAR ON A BARBELL ]

**3. PROPERLY FINISH THE EXERCISE.** We've seen this one over and over: some big meathead feels the need to slam the dumbbells to the floor following a set of presses, attracting *and* distracting everyone in the gym. Not only is he endangering himself, but others as well. There is a safe and quick way of finishing each exercise, and you will learn them. Be disciplined on technique and form, even when ending the set.

**4. USE A SPOTTER ON HEAVY OR RISKY LIFTS.** A spotter is a person, or persons, who stand by to assist during the lift should you need help. If you are trying an exercise for the first time, or if you have just increased the weight, you should use a spotter.

[ USE A SPOTTER! ]

### Guidelines for spotters

- Check the bar for proper loading and collars.
- Know the number of reps to be attempted.
- Help with lift-off and racking of weights, if necessary.
- Motivate your partner!
- Be prepared at all times during the lift to assist if your partner needs it.

**5. MAKE SURE TO RE-RACK ALL OF THE WEIGHTS.** It is the pet peeve of every gym staff to see a weight room full of plates, dumbbells and bars lying on the floor. As a courtesy to the next lifter, and as a very important safety point, please re-rack all.

*"Bicycle racers love living on the edge. They need to know the extremes of their physical limitations, and enjoy living beyond them."*

*—Eric Heiden*
*Olympic speed skating gold medalist, and professional road racer*

[ BE SURE TO PUT ALL EQUIPMENT BACK ]

## RULE NO. 2

### THE BASIS OF ALL IMPROVEMENT IS OVERLOAD

Weight training has many principles that need to be followed in order to stay injury free and to achieve optimum results. The first, and one of the most important, is simple: overload. The overload principle is the foundation of strength training. Simply put, the overload principle states that a muscle will get stronger and more fatigue-resistant when it is called upon to lift more weight than it is normally used to lifting. If the muscle is given the proper amount of overload, and the proper amount of rest, the muscle will increase in strength. (See GAS Principle in Chapter 9).

Getting stronger doesn't necessarily mean getting bigger. A muscle can become stronger in many ways. Muscle hypertrophy is an increase in a muscle's cross-sectional area, this is what body builders do to get bigger and stronger. Endurance athletes should not participate in the typical "bodybuilding" weight-training program that is designed to increase muscle size and strength. Too much muscle mass may potentially harm performance on the bike, although the risk of an endurance athlete bulking up too much is minimal, at best. Whatever weight is gained from resistance training will be greatly offset by the increases in strength and power.

Increasing strength without significantly increasing muscle size occurs by increasing the neural facilitation—the amount of motor units—that fire during a muscle contraction. The more motor units that fire during a muscle contraction, the more force that particular muscle can generate. At the early stages of any weight-training program, the gains in strength are due mainly to this increased neural facilitation.

In order to take complete advantage of the overload principle, make sure that you are overloading your muscles in the appropriate manner. Progression of overload is very important to the overall success of your program. Progressive overload is the systematic increase in frequency, volume and intensity of your weight-training program. The progression of overload in weight training is called **Progressive Resistance Exercise (PRE)**, and it makes up fundamental rule No. 3.

## RULE NO. 3
## CONTINUALLY CHALLENGE YOURSELF

*"If you never confront climbs, you're missing the essence
of the sport. With ascents come adversity. Without adversity, there's
no challenge. Without challenge, no improvement, no sense of
accomplishment, no deep-down joy."*
—*Betsy King*
*U.S. road racer and coach*

Throughout evolution, human beings have had many important attributes that have allowed them to stay on top of the food chain. In order to survive, human beings have had to constantly adapt to their surroundings. Be it growing stronger to perform greater work tasks, running faster to escape predators, or gaining the endurance to live nomadically and travel great distances in search of food and water, humankind has made the necessary adaptations to stay alive and flourish. The human body has always had the ability to adjust to stresses that are placed upon it.

As the body adapts to a stress placed upon it that stress tends to be less apparent. Take for example moving into a house next to a set of railroad tracks. At first the noise of the train drives you crazy, and then, over time, you no longer pay attention to the sound. Your body has adapted to the stress of the noise and it really does not stress you out anymore. Two other examples include the dock worker who has built up huge muscles as an adaptation to moving heavy objects day after day, and the Kenyan schoolboy who has developed incredible endurance from running many miles to school everyday from his village. By applying this overload principle to resistance training, one can learn a valuable lesson in proper program design.

As your body adapts to the "stress" during weight training, you will reach a plateau in your strength improvements. In order to get out of the strength plateau, you must continually change your work-outs. The basic concept of changing your work-outs over time rather than lifting the standard three sets of 10 reps is called **Progressive Resistance Exercise**. This concept has been around for a long time and has been studied from many different aspects, but it all started after World War II.

Researchers in rehabilitation medicine following World War II devised a method of resistance training to improve the strength of soldiers' injured limbs. Their method involved incorporating three sets of exercises each consisting of 10 repetitions done consecutively without resting. The first set was done with one-half of the maximum weight that could be lifted 10 times or $1/2$, 10-RM (repetition maximum, or the maximum amount of weight that one can lift); the second set was done with $3/4$, 10-RM; the final set with the maximum weight (10-RM). As patients trained and became stronger, it was necessary to increase the 10-RM resistance periodically so that strength improvement would continue to progress. The technique of Progressive Resistance Exercise (PRE) is a practical example of the overload principle, and is the basis for most strength training programs today.

Following PRE properly means that, in time, the weight or repetitions of a particular exercise must be increased in order to continue to see improvements in strength and endurance. The amount by which you increase is the key to getting the best results. The recommended amount of increase is approximately 2.5 to 5 percent per week. Once you reach your target for reps you must increase the resistance during the following workout week.

## RULE NO. 4
## SPECIFICITY OF TRAINING IS CRUCIAL
## FOR BEST RESULTS

**R**esistance training follows another cardinal rule of exercise physiology, which is the principle of **Specific Adaptations to Imposed Demands** (SAID). Specificity is the foundation of the SAID principle. In order to receive the most sport-specific benefits from a strength-training program, the program must mirror the demands of the activity that you are trying to improve.

When training to improve riding performance, participation in a typical bodybuilder's program that only incorporates slow isotonic movements, will result in typical "bodybuilders" muscles that are big and slow. Therefore, in order to get the most out of the time you spend weight lifting, you must make the training program cycling-specific. In addition to selecting the proper exercises based on the energy demands of the sport, one needs to look at creating a program that breaks down each exercise for best results. In cycling, the hip joint only moves from 30 to 80 degrees of extension. So, for example, in doing squats, you do not need to go all of the way down to parallel to receive the most desirable results in your cycling-specific program. Squat down only until you have approximately 80 degree bend at the knees, which will simulate the bend in your leg at the top of the pedal stroke.

Speed of movement is also important in your program. Strong muscles from a bodybuilder's program will not make you a faster rider. You also need to train the nervous system. If you want to improve your ability to sprint and create power on the bike, you need to perform power exercises. Adding plyometrics and power cleans into a yearly training program will give you the power results desired. These advanced exercises should be added to the program prior to the racing season, and will be covered in Chapter 7.

## RULE NO. 5
## OBSERVE THE APPROPRIATE REST PERIODS

Focusing on proper rest periods between sets and between work-outs is critical in order to achieve superior results. If you do not rest enough between sets, the muscles will not receive sufficient time to regenerate the energy required for the next set. Adenosine triphosphate (ATP) is the primary energy source for your muscles during weight training, and your body has the ability to regenerate it very quickly. Ninety percent of a muscle's ATP storage will be regenerated after 90 seconds of recovery. In order to properly follow a program designed to maximize strength gains, one should rest at least 90, but no more than 180 seconds between sets. Certain routines, such as circuit training and super sets, require shorter rest periods. Never recuperate more than 180 seconds between sets, as your body will begin to cool down.

In addition to waiting the appropriate time between sets it is necessary, for best results, to rest the suitable time between workouts utilizing the same muscle groups. Muscle tissue is actually damaged on the microscopic level following a weight training work-out and needs to recover before the next lifting session. The minimum amount of time a muscle needs to recover is 48 hours with the rest time not to exceed 72 hours. Waiting too long will diminish results, and not waiting long enough will lead to overtraining. Proper recovery is dependent upon many things: increased riding time, race season, not enough sleep and outside stress.

Listen to your body for the signs of inadequate recovery. Being overtrained leads to excessive muscle soreness and low-quality work-outs. Be careful when combining weight training and cycling as it is easy to become overtrained. On days of heavy lifting, cycling should be a low-intensity effort, and vice-versa.

## WHAT HAPPENS WHEN YOU DON'T REST ENOUGH BETWEEN WORK-OUTS?

If you don't obey the rule of taking adequate rest between each work-out, or if you just plain overdo it, you will be left with some pretty sore muscles. Delayed-onset muscle soreness (DOMS) can be produced by many types of muscular activities. It is most frequently caused by downhill running, lowering heavy weights and plyometrics.

The muscle contractions needed for these types of movements are called eccentric contractions. These movements produce tension as the muscles are forced to lengthen while firing. An eccentric contraction creates an unusually large force on each individual muscle fiber, which can cause sporadic damage and inflammation. While all activities involve some eccentric actions, weight training is one of those that causes the most soreness.

## WHAT CAUSES SORENESS?

Movements that cause muscle soreness have been shown to produce localized damage to the muscle fiber membranes and contractile elements. Chemical irritants, such as histamine, are released from damaged muscles and can irritate pain receptors in the muscle. Muscle damage often causes a swelling of the muscle tissue, which creates enough pressure to stimulate pain receptors. This soreness is a sign from the pain receptors that you have done too much.

Popular explanations for muscle soreness include lactic acid build-up, muscle spasms or muscle damage. Build-ups of lactic acid occur during periods of decreased oxygen availability to the muscle cells, which results in muscular fatigue rather than muscle soreness. However, high levels of lactic acid build-up can stimulate pain receptors immediately following exercise. Muscle spasms (cramps) are reflex reactions caused by trauma of the musculoskeletal system. The two types of spasms are clonic, with involuntary rapid contractions, and tonic, with severe muscle contraction that lasts for a period of time. Clonic spasms, if not relieved quickly, can lead to soreness due to tissue damage.

The leading cause of soreness however, is muscle damage. As previously stated, there is a certain degree of fiber damage that occurs when muscles are overloaded. This natural process of healing and building is part of the adaptation to the physical stress of training.

The initial soreness experienced during the beginning of a weight-training program is normal. If this soreness continues over time it should be considered as a sign of overtraining. Remember that muscle soreness is a sign that your muscles have been worked hard, and need time to recover. Muscle stiffness is different from, but may accompany, muscle soreness. The difference is that true muscle stiffness does not cause pain. It occurs after a muscle group has been pushed to the limit repeatedly. Fluids collect in the muscles during and following exercise. Then, these fluids are absorbed into the bloodstream very slowly, resulting in a muscle that is swollen, shorter, thicker and resistant to stretching. Treatments must center on improving the rate of fluid removal and restoring muscle elasticity.

## TREATMENT OF SORENESS

It is guaranteed that at some point in your weight-training program, you will be a sore puppy, especially after cleans and plyometrics. If you are an athlete, a part of you probably likes being sore. You may think of it as a sign that you've been working hard. This is true, but keep in mind the difference between working hard and working *too* hard. You can choose to walk funny for a few days, or you can do some things to speed up the recovery process. Listed below are some recommendations for the treatment of muscle soreness:
- Light aerobic activity (walking, cycling)
- Gentle stretching
- Sports massage
- Hot bath or Jacuzzi
- Ibuprofen or other anti-inflammatory drugs

*Note: These are recommended treatments to relieve sore-
ness, not injury. If you suffer a muscle pull or joint injury from
overdoing it, the initial application of ice along with compression and elevation is in order. Heat and massage are con-
traindicated for a fresh injury. See a physician or athletic
trainer for further evaluation and treatment advice.*

The only true cure for DOMS is time and prevention. In
Chapter 8 we cover the importance of the recovery process,
and what you can do to further enhance it.

## RULE NO. 6
## HAVE A COMPREHENSIVE BLUEPRINT
## AND STICK TO IT

*"An intelligent plan is the first step to success.
The person who plans knows where he is going, knows
what progress he is making and has a pretty
good idea when he will arrive."*
—Basil Walsh, American Businessman

**M**ost people don't plan to fail they just fail to plan. In
order to get the best results from your program, you
most have a year-round plan that is easy to understand and
easy to stick with. By following the charts and worksheets
provided, you will develop a personalized program designed
to have you peaking in time for next racing season.

## RULE NO. 7
## TRACK YOUR PROGRESS

If you have had trouble sticking with a weight-training program in the past, one of the reasons may have been that you did not have a comprehensive work-out journal. In order to get the best results from your weight training, a well thought out journal is a necessity. One of the great things about having a personal trainer or individual coach is that they will set up and provide a journal for you. If you are not one to keep accurate records, or do not have access to a good trainer or coach, now is the time to change. One of the best ways to reach goals is to have a complete log to record and review your training.

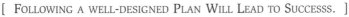

[ FOLLOWING A WELL-DESIGNED PLAN WILL LEAD TO SUCCESSS. ]

*"We need to know where we are going, and how we plan to get there. Our dreams and aspirations must be translated into real and tangible goals, with priorities and a time frame. All of this should be in writing, so that it can be reviewed, updated and revised as necessary."*

—Merlin Olsen, former NFL player

A training journal does not need to be incredibly extensive to be effective. Many of the preprinted training logs available on the market are ridiculously involved. It is easier to file long-form taxes than fill out the pages in some of these journals. Your personal log may be as simple as a spiral notebook or daily calendar. Those of you who are computer wizzes may want to print out sheets with columns for information. Whatever the case, take a few moments after each work-out to record what you did on that day. A journal can be motivating as it keeps you accountable for each training day, and allows you to see your progress over a long period.

The following are things that should be included in your log:

**1. A SECTION FOR YOUR SHORT- AND LONG-TERM GOALS.** Make sure to have a space to chronicle a few goals for each work-out.

**2. A PLACE TO RECORD YOUR WARM-UP AND STRETCH TIME.** Just by having a space to check off that you completed this will help you increase your adherence to quality stretching.

**3. ENOUGH SPACE TO WRITE EACH EXERCISE PERFORMED.** There should be enough room to record number of sets and repetitions.

**4. MAKE SURE TO JOT DOWN FEELINGS.** Note your overall state as well as any injuries on that day before, during and after the work-out.

**5. DON'T FORGET THE CARDIO.** You may keep a separate journal for cycling, or you may choose to keep it all in one. Whatever the case, be sure to track all cardiovascular work and cross-training.

One great thing about keeping an accurate training log is that it can be critiqued in order to figure out problems that you may be experiencing with your training. Have you been consistently overtraining, undertraining, lifting too heavy, too light, or is there not enough variety in your program? Many performance-related questions can be answered just by a careful review of a carefully filled-out exercise log.

*Note: I had to submit my training logs as evidence when I went to court for a settlement after being hit by a car. The logs documented my recovery problems and decreased race performances during the following season due to back pain. I'm glad that I kept good records.—Ken*

**RULE NO. 8**

**BE EFFICIENT DURING YOUR ENTIRE WORKOUT**

Most cyclists do not have that much time to spend on weight training, and the vast majority would rather be out on the bike. Recent research has revealed good news about the amount of time needed to perform an effective routine. In order to get the muscle strengthening benefits that will help your cycling, expect to spend no more than about one hour, two to four times per week in the gym or at home lift-ing weights. For sport-specific weight training, work-out in-tensity and quality are more important than excessive time spent pumping iron. If you are very short on time, here are a few pointers to help you to get more out of the time spent weight training:

1. **FOCUS ON THE CYCLING-SPECIFIC EXERCISES ONLY.** Don't waste time pumping up your chest by perform-ing five sets on the bench press. Stick to the cycling-specific muscle groups when selecting your exercises.

2. **USE EXERCISES THAT WORK NUMEROUS JOINTS WHENEVER POSSIBLE.** Most single-joint exercises aren't as functional as the multi-joint lifts. You will benefit more by do-ing multijoint exercises. For example, if you are pressed for time, choose squats over leg curls.

3. **ADOPT CIRCUIT TRAINING OR SUPER SETS INTO YOUR ROUTINE.** These specialized training styles minimize down time between exercises, therefore limiting the time spent resting between sets.

4. **ALWAYS KNOW WHAT YOU ARE GOING TO DO BE-FORE YOU DO IT.** Never start a work-out without having an idea of what you want to accomplish. Go into the gym with a plan, and stick to it.

## RULE NO. 9
### STABILIZE! STABILIZE! STABILIZE!

To get better muscle isolation and to reduce the risk of in-jury, proper stabilization during your weight training should be of prime concern. Stabilization refers to being able to hold the proper body positions in relation to the reference "ready" position. Lifting without the ability to stabilize your body is like riding a bike without a strong frame. You might be able to ride it for a while, but eventually the weak, unstable frame will lead to major problems.

In order to stabilize your body properly, work on your core stabilization. Making up the core of your body are the muscles along the spine, scapular muscles and abdominal region. After developing the ability to properly stabilize the core, you will be able to move on to the more advanced exercises that require a greater amount of stabilization to perform safely. One of the best ways to think about proper stabilization is to remember to stabilize the joint closest to the one you are working. For example, focus on stabilization of the shoulder joint when doing biceps curls.

## RULE NO. 10
## GREAT RESULTS COME WITH
## PATIENCE AND PERFECT PRACTICE

*"Repeated actions are stored as habits. If the repeated actions aren't fundamentally sound, then what comes out in a game can't be sound. What comes out will be bad habits."*
*— Chuck Knox, NFL coach*

As great as weight training can be for improving cycling performance, it can be equally effective at injuring you if performed incorrectly. In order to minimize potential injuries, you need to adopt the proper postures required for each exercise. Just as there is an optimum position on the bike, there is also an optimum position to performing every weight-training exercise. Optimum positioning for lifting starts out in what will be refered to as the weight-training "ready" position.

In order to get in the proper ready position, you need to understand the term, neutral position. Neutral position refers to the position of the body often seen on the small illustrations posted on most weight-training machines. In this position, the body is centered, weight is equally balanced over the feet, knees are slightly bent, the spine has its normal curves, shoulders are held slightly back and down, the head is properly positioned with the ears above the shoulders, and the eyes are looking forward. This neutral position is extremely important for everyone that trains with weights. It is in this position that the body is most stable and resistant to injury.

## THE TOP-10 WEIGHT-TRAINING MISTAKES:

**1. OVERDOING IT.** This is probably the most common mistake with cyclists, and other athletes, who add weight training to their routines. Having a very strong cardiovascular system doesn't set you up to be able to lift at a level of high intensity. Remember that your training follows the law of specificity. Do not try to rush into the intense phases of the program or else you and your muscles will be sorry.

**2. NOT BEING CONSISTENT AND/OR PATIENT.** As with anything worthwhile, good things come to those who are steady and diligent. Consistently sticking to a periodized program will lead to great results. Training for quick results with weights does not work. Remember, strength gained quickly is lost quickly, and strength which is gained slowly will be lost slowly.

**3. ALLOWING HIPS TO LIFT OFF THE PAD DURING A LEG-PRESS MOVEMENT.** This is a $10,000 mistake. By letting your hips come off of the pad at the bottom of the leg-press movement, you are setting yourself up for a ruptured disk (back surgery runs around $10,000). Repeatedly putting yourself in this risky position allows your lower back disks to be one step away from a total blow-out. Maintain a neutral spine during the entire range of motion of any leg-press movement.

**4. NOT KEEPING YOUR SPINE IN THE NEUTRAL POSITION.** In addition to the leg press mentioned above, all other exercises require the back to be kept in the neutral position. The only exceptions are some of the abdominal exercises in which a flat low back is necessary for complete abdominal recruitment.

**5. NOT LIFTING ENOUGH WEIGHT.** Believe it or not, this is a mistake made all too often. Following your program and truly lifting at the proper intensity are necessary for maximizing strength. Make sure that if the program states to lift three sets of eight reps, that the weight is heavy enough so that you are hard-pressed to finish the last rep.

**6. SQUATTING WITH IMPROPER FORM.** The squat is a very important lift, and the foundation of the lower body exercises. Many people think they are performing squats correctly only if they "go all the way down." As you will learn in the next chapter, it is not necessary to perform a full squat to improve cycling-specific strength. Once proper technique is learned, the squat is a fun and challenging exercise.

**7. GOING FOR THE STRETCH WITH THE BENCH PRESS.** One of the common mistakes made when lifting with the upper body is to think that the bar should come all the way down to the chest during the bench press. For most people, unless they are football linemen, that extreme position is not necessary. It puts an unnecessary strain on the anterior joint capsule of the shoulder. The general rule is to allow the bar to come down only until it is a fist's distance from the chest. By keeping the bar a short distance from the chest you will obtain added safety as well as better results.

**8. PERFORMING EXERCISES TOO FAST.** Lifting in a slow, controlled manner is very important to achieve full benefit from each lift. Early in the program it is crucial to lift at a slow pace to allow the joints, tendons and muscles to adapt to the increasing loads. Later in the program, some lifts will be performed more explosively to increase power output. These exercises are the exception to the rule. Resist the temptation to swing the weights and use momentum to assist your effort. If you adapt this lazy style of quick lifting you are only inviting injury.

**9. PERFORMING PULL-DOWNS BEHIND THE HEAD.** Behind-the-head pull-downs are considered to be "old school" thinking. This motion is very dangerous for your rotator cuff muscles and is unnecessary. Performing the pull-down in front as described in Chapter 6 will give you all of the upper back strength development without risking damage to your shoulders.

**10. PERFORMING OVERHEAD PRESSES BEHIND THE HEAD.** The same line of thinking is true with the overhead press as well. No additional benefit comes from performing overhead presses behind the head. To save your shoulders, please do not ever press weight from behind the head.

## TIPS TO STAYING HEALTHY DURING LIFTING

Every winter, the cold and flu season runs on overdrive, especially in the gym. With so many people indoors coughing and sneezing, and then handling the equipment, it's no wonder that germs spread so rapidly. Take precautions so that you will not lose valuable training time due to falling ill. Here are some practical tips to reduce the risk of illness while working out in a public facility:

• Wash hands frequently. There are too many surfaces that hands come in contact with during a work-out that have the nasties on them.

• Try not to touch hands to face while working out.

• Eat well and get adequate sleep to create the optimum environment for the body to adapt to training.

• Reduce the intensity and duration of work-outs or skip training altogether when symptoms of sickness appear.

• When unsure about whether to train, use the neck-check rule. If the symptoms of illness are above the neck—mild headache, stuffed-up or runny nose, mild sore throat—see how you feel after an easy warm up, then decide whether or not to train. If symptoms are below the neck—congestion deep in the lungs, severe sore throat, fever, persistent coughing, upset stomach, body aches—skip training until the symptoms disappear completely.

• Remain well-hydrated. The dehydration and elevated body temperature that often occur during and after exercise can also suppress the immune system.

## READY FOR THE EXERCISES

Now that you have a good idea of the main "rules" of weight training, and know some things to avoid, it's time to learn the fun stuff: practicing the movements that will be incorporated into a weight-training program. Chapters 4, 5 and 6 cover all of the exercises in the program, dividing them up into lower body, torso and upper body.

# CHAPTER FOUR

# Lower Body Exercises

*"Cyclists worship legs. Your legs carry you over mountains, even when your mind and heart have long since abandoned the cause. Your legs—made solid by the miles—supply tangible evidence of your cycling progress. And your legs are what people notice at the beach."*
—*Nelson Peña*
*renowned cycling writer*

When a cyclist thinks about strength and power on the bike, he or she automatically thinks of legs. Visions of chiseled, cut-up gams of world-class cyclists come to mind: legs that are capable of propelling the rider and the bike, at high speeds, for hours on end, climbing huge mountains, and accelerating to tremendous, instantaneous sprinting speeds. Cyclists love legs, and not just their own. And, heck, half the reason we shave them is to show them off, right?

While the muscles of the lower body—legs and hips—require the assistance of muscles in the rest of the body to move a bike, lower body muscles are primary to the effort. For this reason, and to grab your attention, we are covering lower body exercises first. Most of these exercises are multijoint, meaning that they work the muscles that move more than one joint. Many of them combine hip and knee extension, motions that are specific to pedaling a bike. Your legs and hips are power centers; work them hard and see the results!

*"Motivation can't take you very far if you don't have the legs."*
—*Lance Armstrong*
*1993 world road race champion*

## SQUATS

**S**quats should be the foundation of a weight training for cycling program. They strengthen the majority of the lower body muscles in a very functional movement by simulating the hip and knee extension motions that will drive the bike. This is not a simple exercise, so take note of proper form. Practice with light weights until you are performing the squat perfectly.

- Start with an Olympic bar, evenly loaded with collars.
- Adjust the squat rack so that the bar is at chest level.
- With a spotter, place the bar along your upper back. Avoid putting the bar along your neck.
- Make sure you start in the correct position; back slightly arched, abdominals held tight, feet directly under bar, chest out, and shoulder blades held back.
- Inhale and start the movement, make sure you keep your back from rounding forward, your hips from shifting to one

side, and keep your knees in proper alignment. Align the knees so that you can draw an imaginary line from the middle of the knee caps to the space between the first and second toes.

• Squat down only as far as possible in order to keep good form. Remember not everyone has the proper biomechanics to let them go down to a right angle at their knees. Cyclists only need to squat down until they have about a 80 degree angle at their knee joint—the same as the top of the pedal stroke.

• Exhale while slowly raising the bar.

• Straighten the hips and knees while maintaining proper body position.

• Repeat the exercise the recommended number of reps. Step forward and rerack the weight by squatting down and bending both knees.

## DEAD LIFTS

Dead lifts are a very good exercise to improve the overall lower body strength needed in all aspects of cycling, especially long periods in the aerodynamic position. Pay particular attention to maintaining proper lower back position to avoid injury.

Use of a weight belt is recommended for this exercise.

• Begin with an equally loaded and collared Olympic bar on the ground.

• Use an alternate, slightly wider than shoulder-width, grip with thumbs around the bar.

• Feet should be shoulder-width apart, back is slightly arched and abdominals are held tight throughout.

• Inhale and lift the weight in a slow, controlled manner by extending the knees, moving hips forward and raising shoulders up and back. Keep your head up, facing forward. Make sure to keep the bar close to legs with feet flat on the floor.

• Back stays rigid as hips move forward until knees are under the bar. Torso is vertical and erect.

• Keep shoulder blades back, chest out, and abdominals tight throughout the movement.

• Exhale at the top, pause, and slowly lower the weight back to the floor keeping abdominals tight, maintaining erect torso position.

• It is very important to remember not to round the back at all during the entire movement.

## LEG PRESS

**T**he leg press is an excellent way to increase lower body strength without putting unwanted compression on the spine. Some people are unable to squat because of back problems and this offers them a good alternative.

• Leg press machines may be plate loaded (as pictured) or utilize a weight stack.

• After evenly loading the machine, place your feet approximately 6 to 18 inches apart.

• Contract your abdominal muscles, inhale, and begin to let the weight down slowly.

• Come down only as far as you can, keeping your hips on the seat. Do not let your hips turn under and come off of the seat pad. Allowing the hips to come off is very dangerous and should be avoided at all costs.

• Exhale as you press the weight back. Push with the whole foot, keeping your knees in proper alignment. You should be able to draw an imaginary line from the kneecap to a spot between the first and second toes.

• Continue pressing until the knees are just short of being locked.

## LUNGES

**L**unges are a great cycling exercise because they work so many of the important muscles of the lower body used in cycling. They help build stabilizing muscles, and by isolating one leg at a time, strengthen any imbalances you may have.

- Start by using only your body weight, then add resistance either on your shoulders with a barbell or by holding dumbbells when you are ready.
- Take a wide split stance, one foot forward, one back, and feet facing forward, parallel to each other.

- With head up and abdominals tight, bend both knees until the back knee almost touches the ground and the front knee is at a 90-degree angle.
- Repeat the exercise with the same leg for the recommended number of repetitions and then switch legs.

*Note: A more advanced lunge is the step-forward lunge. Keeping in mind the previous points, step forward to lunge and then alternate with the other leg each repetition.*

## SINGLE-LEG SQUATS

This exercise is highly recommended to increase leg strength while improving strength imbalances. Since it is a single-leg exercise, you will also improve your balance while utilizing stabilizing muscles.

- Begin by using just your body weight, adding resistance with dumbbells when you are ready.

- Stand upright with one leg behind supported by a chair or bench. Squat downward by bending both legs keeping the torso upright, abdominals held tight, and chest out.

- Lower your body down until you have approximately an 80-degree bend in the front knee. Extend upward and repeat recommended number of repetitions.

- Repeat the exercise with the other leg forward, and rest when you have completed both legs.

*Note: Do not let the front knee go too far out over the toe.*

## STEP-UPS

**S**teps-ups, as with the single-leg squat, work on individual leg strength, exercising the hamstrings, quadriceps and the gluteals all in one exercise. Do not perform this exercise if you have kneecap pain.

• Select a bench that is high enough to give you about a 90-degree bend in the knee as you step up.

• Begin by using only your body weight, and add resistance with either dumbbells or a barbell when you are ready.

• Step-up on the bench with one foot. Pushing with the heel and keeping your torso upright, move the other foot up onto the bench.

• Step down in reverse order and repeat the movement with the other leg. Continue in an alternating fashion until the desired number of repetitions are completed.

• Remember to exhale as you step-up, inhale as you step down, keeping your abdominals held tight throughout.

## LEG CURL

**T**he leg curl is a very important exercise for cyclists. Performing the leg curl isolates and strengthens the hamstrings, a muscle group typically underdeveloped compared to the mighty quadriceps. The hamstrings are important in applying upward force on the pedals during sprinting, climbing and track starts.

- Using a leg curl machine, select the appropriate weight, and line your knees up with the axis of rotation of the machine.

- Contract abdominals tightly to keep your hips from lifting off of the pad while you raise your heels toward the gluteals.

- Pause on the top, then slowly lower the weight, keeping the lower back from excessively arching.

- Repeat in a slow, controlled manner the recommended number of repetitions.

## CALF PRESS

**C**yclists are notorious for their well-developed thighs, but have you ever noticed that most successful riders also have exceptional lower leg development as well? Strong calf muscles are essential for efficient transfer of power to the pedals. Performing calf presses is a great way to develop total strength in this muscle group.

• Using a leg press or calf machine, adjust the machine so that your leg is extended with a slight bend in the knee.

• Place your feet so that the balls of each foot are in contact with the pad or platform. With your feet shoulder-width apart, raise the weight by pointing your toes away from you. Pause on the top and then slowly lower the weight.

*Note: Another way to work the calf muscles without any equipment is to perform the calf raise. This exercise is performed*

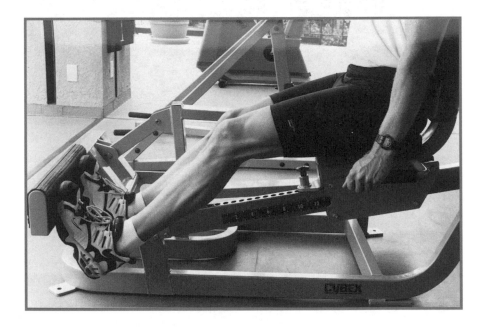

*by standing on the edge of a step and raising your body weight against gravity. The standing calf machine duplicates this motion while allowing added resistance through a weight stack.*

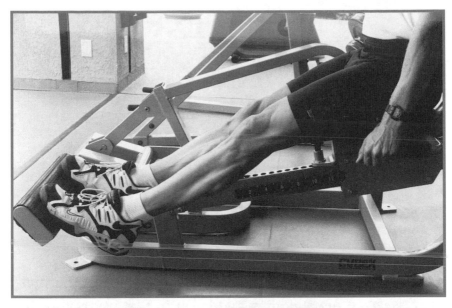

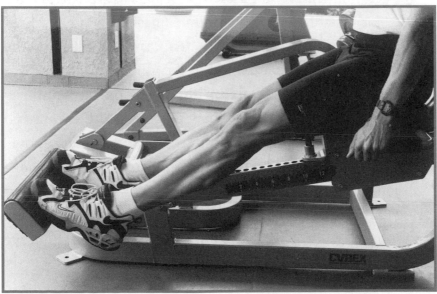

# CHAPTER FIVE

# Trunk
## Exercises

*"Machines don't break records. Muscles do."*
*—Lon Haldeman*
*1982–83 Race Across America winner*

The muscles of the trunk—which consist of the muscles of the abdomen and lower back—are responsible for posture and power transmission while cycling. They are the link between the legs that drive the bike and the upper body muscles that control and connect you to it. Their function in cycling is to stabilize the pelvis on the saddle so that power can be transferred efficiently to the drive train and not be through with extraneous hip and upper body movement. Weight-training programs for cyclists in the past have traditionally neglected the importance of a strong trunk, centering only on developing leg strength. That old school thinking is gone now, so pay attention to this chapter and improve your efficiency and comfort on the bike.

## HIP LIFTS

The hip-lift exercise is a great way to work the lower back, hamstring and gluteal muscles. This pelvic stabilization exercise does not require special equipment, and will prepare you to be safer and more energy efficient during long hours in the saddle. This exercise requires strength and control to perform, so pay close attention to your form.

- Lie on your back with knees bent, feet flat on the floor, and arms resting at your side. Feet are shoulder width apart and directly under the knees.

- Flatten out the arch in your lower back and hold in a "pelvic tilt"—which is performed by pulling the abdominals toward your spine, rotating the hips backward and flattening the lower back against the floor. This creates a safe pelvic position for performing exercises. Then, lift the hips until your body forms a straight line between shoulders and knees.

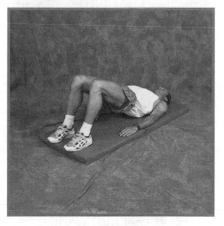

- Keeping thighs parallel to each other, extend one leg out and hold, then slowly lower hips toward the floor, while keeping leg extended and hips level.

• Reach the point of almost touching the floor, then push the supporting foot into the ground, lifting back up to the starting position.

• Repeat the recommended number of repetitions and then move on to the other leg.

## BACK EXTENSIONS

**K**eeping a strong lower back will help you avoid injury and ride more comfortably for extended periods of time. The lumbar muscles assist the abdominal muscles in holding the pelvis stable while in the bent-over riding position. Their actions are crucial to efficient power transfer between your upper and lower body. In addition to working the spinal erectors, this exercise also strengthens hamstrings and gluteals.

• Using a back extension bench, start with your body extended into a straight position, arms crossed at chest. A weight plate may be held at your chest to add resistance as you progress.

• Keep your back in a non-rounded (neutral) position during the entire exercise.

• Lower your body toward the floor continuing the movement as far down as possible in order to maintain the neutral back position.

• At the bottom, concentrate on activation of the gluteals and hamstrings forcing them to help out the lumbar muscles as you raise back up into the starting position.

*Note: Perform this exercise carefully. If you feel any lower back discomfort, stop immediately. If you have a history of lower back problems, perform the following prone cobra exercise for a few weeks before adding back extensions.*

## PRONE COBRA

The prone cobra works the lower and upper extensor muscles of the spine. These muscles are utilized in many facets of cycling from holding an aerodynamic tuck to bunny hopping a log off-road.

• Begin by lying on your stomach looking down toward the floor with arms at your sides, thumbs turned out and up.

• Tighten the gluteal muscles and extend off of the floor by "peeling" yourself up slowly (5-10 seconds). Pause at the top, then slowly lower back down.

• Perform the appropriate number of repetitions, then rest.

## ABDOMINALS

The muscles of the abdominal region can be divided into three groups: lower, upper and obliques (sides). For this reason, we present abdominal exercises designed to target each of these three areas.

We recommend that you always begin your abdominal work with an exercise that isolates the lower abdominals. The reason for this is that the lower abs require the most effort and coordination to perform properly.

All floor abdominal exercises are performed with bent knees, and begin with a "pelvic tilt" (see "Hip lifts).

## KNEE RAISE—REVERSE CRUNCH

The knee raise and reverse crunch are excellent exercises to isolate the muscles of the lower abdomen.

### THE KNEE RAISE

- Start by lying on your back with legs up, knees bent at 90 degrees, and thighs perpendicular to the floor.

- Maintaining a flat back, allow your legs to extend outward as far as possible without arching the lower back upward. For some people, this may be only a few inches.

Then, bring your knees to your chest, concentrating on the lower abdominal area throughout the entire movement.

• Perform this exercise at a steady, controlled pace. Do not rock or swing to use momentum to help.

• Breathe normally throughout the set, performing the appropriate number of repetitions.

## REVERSE CRUNCH

**A** more advanced version of the knee raise—or reverse crunch—is performed on a slant board or decline bench to add more gravity resistance.

• Start by lying on your back with legs up, knees bent at 90 degrees, and thighs perpendicular to the floor.

• Maintaining a flat back and keeping a 90-degree angle at

the knee joint, bring knees back to your chest. Pause at the top, concentrating on the lower abdominal area throughout the entire movement.

• Perform this exercise at a steady, controlled pace. Do not rock or swing to use momentum to help.

• Breathe normally throughout the set, performing the appropriate number of repetitions.

## OBLIQUE CRUNCHES

This exercise is used to isolate the oblique muscles that lie across the sides of the trunk and torso. These muscles allow for the actions of twisting and side bending of the trunk.

• Begin by lying on your

back with unlaced fingers
supporting your head. As-
sume the pelvic tilt position
with feet flat on the floor (basic) or legs raised with knees
bent 90 degrees (advanced).

• Rise up diagonally, keeping elbows back. Bring one
shoulder blade completely off of the floor, alternate sides and
repeat motion to fatigue.

**Note:** *For increased resistance, a slant board may be utilized when performing this exercise.*

## ABDOMINAL CRUNCHES

**T**he abdominal crunch has replaced the traditional sit-up as
the most basic abdominal exercise to perform. The major
difference between the two exercises is that the crunch is

performed by raising high enough to lift your shoulder blades off the floor, while the sit-up involves raising all of the way up to your knees. The crunch is more effective in isolating the abdominals, while sit-ups utilize the hip flexor muscles to complete the motion.

• Begin by lying on your back with unlaced fingers supporting your head. Assume the pelvic tilt position with feet flat on the floor (basic) or legs raised with knees bent 90 degrees (advanced).

• Make sure to keep your elbows back, chin off your chest, and back flat throughout the movement. Imagine there is an orange between your chin and chest, and gently hold it there.

• While looking at the ceiling, curl up until your shoulder blades lift off of the floor, pause for a moment, then lower.

• Do not pull up on your head with your hands or bring elbows inward during the exercise.

• Be sure not to hold your breath, and perform slow, controlled repetitions to fatigue.

# CHAPTER SIX

# Upper Body Exercises

*"It's hard to measure yourself if nobody is challenging you."*
*—John Tomac*
*U.S. professional mountain-bike racer*

An area often neglected by riders, the upper body, needs to be strengthened throughout the year to improve overall bike performance. A strong upper body is essential for effective power transfer, controlled steering and braking, and safety in the event of a crash. For mountain bikers, the importance of developing a strong upper body that can endure many miles of rough terrain is more important than ever.

In the past, cyclists have wanted nothing more than to lose upper body weight to help make them better climbers. Today, with the majority of North American road racers competing almost exclusively in criteriums, upper body development is less of a hindrance and more of an asset. Power is essential in criterium racing due to the aggressive style and amount of sprinting that is involved. Even if you are a road racer, do not shy away from doing any upper body strengthening; you will need to stand up to climb sometime.

The focus of modern strength-training programs for cyclists centers around development of strength without adding bulk. By following a program that emphasizes lower body and trunk development, the building of unwanted upper body mass is less likely to occur.

## THE ROTATOR CUFF

The shoulder is a ball-and-socket joint. Unfortunately, the ball (head of the humerus) does not sit in the socket (glenoid fossa) very deeply, and most of the stability of the joint must be provided by muscles, tendons and ligaments. The group of four muscles that holds the arm in its socket is called the *rotator cuff*. These muscles lay underneath the deltoids, and are crucial to proper function of the shoulder joint. Keeping them strong is your best protection in the case of a fall, and will help you recover more quickly following an injury.

These three exercises are very simple, do not take long to perform, and make for a good warm-up prior to working your upper body. Combine these exercises with the upper body stretches in this book to improve the function and stability of your shoulders.

### RESISTANCE BAND EXTERNAL ROTATION

This exercise strengthens the muscles that laterally rotate the shoulder. With so many daily activities requiring arms to be in front of you in an internally rotated position—including cycling—it is very important to maintain the strength of the external rotators.

- Attach a resistance band at shoulder height and stand at a right angle while grasping the handle with thumb pointing upward.

- Stabilize elbow against your side and pull the cord outward as far as possible without twisting your body, pause, then return to the starting position.

## DUMBBELL EXTERNAL ROTATION

This is a more advanced version of the above exercise. It may be substituted for the resistance cord exercise, but you should do both if you have a history of shoulder problems.

- Lie on your side, holding a dumbbell in your upside arm. With your arm bent 90 degrees and palm facing downward, raise the dumbbell by rotating your arm outward, keeping elbow at your side.

- Raise the dumbbell only as far as possible without twist-

ing your body, then slowly lower to the starting position. Perform a set, and then switch to the other side.

## EMPTY CANS

This exercise gets its name from the motion that resembles someone "emptying two cans" by holding them out to the sides upside down. This exercise isolates the very important, and often ruptured, supraspinatus muscle of the rotator cuff.

• Begin in a standing position, shoulders back and head up. Hold dumbbells at sides in an internally rotated position, thumbs down.

• Slowly raise the dumbbells in a plane that is approximately 30 degrees forward of straight to the sides. Stop below shoulder level, then slowly lower to the starting position.

## BENCH PRESS

The bench press is a great upper body exercise that will increase overall strength, and give you more stability and control when in a tough steering situation. This exercise can be performed using either Olympic bar or dumbbells, and on a flat or incline bench. The use of an incline bench emphasizes more of the upper pectoral muscles, but may not be recommended for people with shoulder problems. The use of a spotter is recommended.

## OLYMPIC BENCH PRESS

• With a spotter and evenly weighted bar with collars, lie on bench, grip with the thumbs around the bar spaced evenly from the center and slightly wider than shoulder width.

• With feet on the floor, tighten abdominals and gluteals. Inhale and lower the bar slowly, keeping elbows out at your sides until they are slightly below shoulder level. Do not bounce the bar on your chest!

• Exhale as you press the bar up. Keep your chest up, shoulder blades down and back throughout the move-

ment. At the top position, do not lock elbows.

• Repeat the recommended number of repetitions.

## DUMBBELL BENCH PRESS

This exercise is essentially the same as the Olympic bench press, only with dumbbells rather than a barbell. The main difference between the two is that dumbbells require the use of more stabilizing muscles and are, therefore, a slightly more functional exercise. Also, the use of dumbbells may place less stress on the shoulder joint by allowing more freedom of motion.

• Start with the dumbbells in a straight line, arms directly above shoulders. Chest is out, shoulder blades pinched back and down, start the lowering motion with your elbows going straight out to the sides. Bend at your elbow keeping wrists above them during the entire movement.

• Exhale as you push up, pause at the top, and slowly repeat the motion.

Caution! With this exercise, it is very easy to lower the dumbbells too far and over stretch the anterior joint capsule of your shoulder. Remember, the weights are only lowered until the elbows are slightly below shoulder level, no more.

## PULL-DOWNS

The pull-down exercise works the entire upper back and biceps. These muscles are necessary for sprinting and out-of-the-saddle climbing when you will need to pull on the handlebars with great force.

Current research suggests that there is no added benefit by performing this exercise by pulling the bar down behind your head. This position has shown to be potentially dangerous to the neck and shoulders and is being phased out of most programs.

• Sit at the machine and adjust the pads so they rest on your thighs when your feet are flat on the floor. After adjusting the machine to the appropriate weight, grasp a straight bar with an overhand grip a little wider than shoulder width.

• Start the movement by pulling the shoulder blades down, then move elbows out to continue the motion.

• Only pull down far enough so that your forearm stays in a straight line parallel with the cable that is attached to the bar (usually chin level).

• Exhale on the pull-down, pause, and then slowly

lower the weight. Repeat the movement without letting the weights hit the stack.

## PULL-UPS

**P**ull-ups do not require any fancy equipment and can be done almost anywhere that there is a strong, horizontal bar overhead. This exercise works the same muscles as the pull-downs.

• Grasp the bar overhead with an overhand grip and hands slightly wider than shoulder width apart. Slowly pull yourself up exhaling throughout the pull until your chin clears the bar.

• Pause at the top for a moment, then slowly lower yourself down to complete extension of the arms.

*Note: Most gyms now have machines, such as the Gravitron, which utilize air pressure or a weight stack to assist in lifting a percentage of your total body weight. These machines offer three different hand positions and are a great way to progress to a full-body-weight pull-ups.*

## ONE ARM DUMBBELL ROW

**T**he one arm dumbbell row is an excellent upper-back exercise that can easily be performed with home gym equipment. This functional movement builds muscles that mountain bikers use to jump obstacles, and all cyclists use for out-of-the-saddle efforts.

• Start by kneeling on a flat bench with one foot on the ground, and the opposite hand resting on the bench for support. Back should be flat and parallel to the floor.

• With the dumbbell safely placed on the ground, begin by picking it up as if you were going to start a lawn mower.

• With the dumbbell hanging at full arm extension, start by pinching your shoulder blade and then continue pulling, keeping your wrist under your elbow until elbow reaches your torso.

• Do not allow your body to tilt, or back to rise, from flat position while lifting. Keep your abs tight, and do not swing the weight.

• Pause on the top with your chest out, shoulder blades squeezed down and back. Then, slowly lower to the starting position.

• Repeat the recommended number of repetitions, and then, move on to the next arm.

## CABLE ROW

The cable row works the muscles of the upper back, posterior shoulder and biceps.

• This exercise may be performed on a cable row machine or using any machine that offers a low pulley.

• Sit with your knees slightly bent with feet on the base of machine or foot supports. Torso is perpendicular to the floor and arms are extended forward, hands grasping the handle.

• Exhale as you engage the upper-back muscles, pinching shoulder blades together as you pull the handle toward your body. Do not lean backward while pulling.

• Once the handle reaches your chest, pause briefly, then, slowly straighten arms to lower the weight, keeping elbows at your sides. Be careful not to round your back.

*Note: Many gyms have a specific weight stack machine for performing a very similar exercise. **Machine rows** utilize a seat and chest pad to lock you into position, and thus are safer for people with lower back problems. Both will work the upper back, but the cable row will use your lower back muscles for stability—something important for cyclists.*

## DUMBBELL SHRUGS

The shrug exercise develops the upper trapezius (these attach at the base of the neck, and help hold your melon up while in the cycling position). These muscles often get tired during long rides and time trials, which can lead to great discomfort. Remember, a stronger muscle is more resistant to fatigue.

• Start in a standing position with feet shoulder width apart, knees slightly bent, and abdominals tight.

• Holding a dumbbell in each hand with arms straight, slowly elevate shoulders with a shrugging motion as if you were saying, "I don't know." Pause at the top, then slowly let the shoulders drop down, lowering the weights to the starting position.

• Exhale as you lift up, keeping the abs tight. Inhale as you let the weight back down.

• Make sure not to move your shoulders in a circle as this puts them at an unnecessary risk of injury.

## DUMBBELL SHOULDER PRESSES

**H**aving strong shoulders will help you be able to have more control on the bike, especially on off-road descents.

• Perform this exercise while seated in a sturdy chair or adjustable bench set at 90 degrees, with feet planted firmly on the floor.

• Hold a dumbbell in each hand at ear level with palms forward. Exhale as you push the dumbbells up and inward overhead.

• Pause on the top and slowly bring the weight back down.

*Note: Do not perform with a barbell behind the head as this puts the shoulders in a position of unnecessary risk.*

There are three additional dumbbell exercises that can be performed to further strengthen the shoulders to improve bike control. These dumbbell exercises isolate different parts of the deltoid muscle and consist of front raises, lateral raises and rear shoulder raises.

## FRONT RAISES

This exercise isolates the anterior deltoid muscle.

• Stand with feet shoulder width apart, knees slightly bent, tight abdominals, chest out, shoulders back, head forward and elbows soft.

• Alternate arms lift one dumbbell at a time out in front at a slight angle, pausing when the dumbbell reaches shoulder level.

• Exhale as you lift, and inhale as the weight comes slowly back to the starting position, being sure not to lean or arch your back.

## LATERAL RAISES

This exercise works the middle section of your shoulder muscles and may be substituted for overhead presses if you suffer from rotator cuff problems.

• Stand with your feet shoulder width apart, knees slightly bent, tight abdominals, chest out, shoulders back, head forward and elbows soft.

• Hold the dumbbells with palms inward, then raise both arms at the same time, lifting out to the sides at a slight angle, pausing when the dumbbell reaches just below the level of your shoulders.

• Imagine that there are strings attached to your elbows and they are leading the activity, not your wrists.

• Exhale as you lift, and inhale as the weight comes slowly back to the starting position.

## REAR SHOULDER RAISES

This exercise works the muscles on the back of the shoulder.

• Lying face down on an incline bench set at about 30 degrees, hold the dumbbells with palms facing rearward and arms extended below.

• Leading the motion with your elbows, lift the dumbbells

out to the sides of you at a 90-degree angle , pausing when the dumbbell reaches shoulder level.

• Make sure to keep wrists under your elbows throughout the entire lift.

• Exhale as you lift, and inhale as the weight comes slowly back to the starting position.

## DIPS

Dips are a great upper body exercise because they do not require fancy equipment. They strengthen triceps, which muscles needed for shock absorption in all cycling, especially on steep off-road descents.

• Grasp the parallel bars of a triceps dip station while stepping on a block. With arms extended and supporting your body weight, face forward. Knees should be bent with feet together or crossed.

• Slowly bend at the elbow to lower your body, making sure not to go a position below having upper arms parallel to the floor.

• Exhale as you push up, do not lock your arms at the top, pause, and slowly repeat the exercise.

• Try not to bounce at the bottom of the movement.

**Do not perform dips if you have separated your shoulder in the past**!

## TRICEPS EXTENSION
## WITH DUMBBELLS

To handle the bumps of riding and pressure of leaning on the bars, keeping triceps strong is very important. This exercise helps balance the strength in your arms that can greatly improve bike control.

• Start by lying on a flat bench with arms straightened, weights directly over shoulders, and hands turned inward.

• Bend at the elbows to lower the weights, keeping upper arms still and perpendicular to the bench. Keep abs tight, and do not arch your back.

• Bring the weights down as far as you can without moving upper arms (about ear level). Extend back up, pause and repeat.

## TRICEPS EXTENSIONS WITH HIGH PULLEY

Here is a variation on the triceps extension that utilizes a high pulley. This exercise may be performed using a number of different handles.

• Attach a bar to the cable on a high pulley machine. Grab the bar with an overhand shoulder-width grip, and pull down until your elbows are at your sides.

• Stand tall, keeping elbows at your sides. Press the bar toward your thighs, pause, and then return to the starting position.

• Do not allow shoulders to assist in bringing your arms forward and backward during this exercise.

Variations of this lift include using a rope or V-bar for a handle, or a horseshoe handle for one-handed pushdowns.

## BICEPS CURLS

The biceps are used every time you pull up on handlebars. Obviously, these are muscles that you want to keep strong.

• Standing or seated, hold dumbbells with your wrists turned inward, and arms extended.

• Slowly bend the elbows, twisting your hands to a palms-up position while bringing the weight toward your shoulders.

• Make sure to keep shoulders back and down throughout the entire movement. To maximize fatigue in the biceps, keep elbows at your sides during the motion.

The **hammer curl** is a variation of the biceps curl, which keeps the hands turned inward throughout the whole motion. This exercise simulates the on-the-hoods, or bar-end, positions in cycling.

## WRIST FLEXION-EXTENSION

Keeping the wrists strong is very important in cycling, especially for off-road riding. These exercises will also help increase grip strength, which can be another asset in tough riding situations.

For each exercise, start in a seated position with forearms resting on your thighs.

• For the wrist flexion, hold dumbbells in a palms-up

position with your hands over the edge of your knees. Curl the weight by flexing your wrist, then lower.

• To perform the wrist extension, hold the dumbbells in a palms-down position with hands extended over the edge of your knees. Raise the weight by extending wrist upwards, then lower the weight.

• Do not let forearms raise from your thighs. You may need to start with low weights to perform this exercise correctly.

# CHAPTER SEVEN

# Power
## Development

*"Power. Think about the word. It is what separates casual riders from the elite. You can be a precision bike handler, a wheel-sucker extraordinaire, an elegant pedaler—but if you can't crank when the crunch comes, you'll be left behind."*
—*Fred Matheny*
*renown cycling writer*

How many times have you heard of a successful bike racer referred to as "powerful?" Face it, success in cycling stems greatly from the amount of power a rider is able to apply to the pedals when it is crunch time—in an attack, climb or sprint. When it is time to quickly accelerate the bike, all of those long endurance rides that were logged into your training diary during the winter aren't going to help do the trick. You need to have been performing specific exercises to improve explosiveness if you wish to improve your edge.

Don't get the wrong idea here, we are not saying that muscular endurance and strength aren't just as important to a cyclist's overall development. True, if you do not have the strength and endurance to stay in contention in a race, all of

107

[ A GROUP SPRINT ]

the power in the world won't help. The point is that when you are making a potentially winning move in a breakaway or a sprint, power is what you will need to be successful.

To losely define the word, power is the product of the force exerted on an object and the velocity of the object in the direction in which the force is exerted.

**Power = force x velocity**

Before you have a nasty physics class flashback, let us explain how this relates to you on your bicycle. Power is required to start an object rotating about an axis, or to change the velocity at which it rotates. Thus, to quickly accelerate your bike, you must quickly accelerate the cranks. Be it going from a standstill to top speed. Or, picture Mario Cipollini jumping from 35 to 40 mph in a few pedal strokes. It takes power.

Most of the difficulty in increasing speed is that you must overcome increased air drag. Dr. Edmund Burke states that the power required to overcome air drag is proportional to the cube of the velocity. What this means is to double speed, the power must be increased eight times. Thus, to increase speed from 20 to 25 mph, you must *double* the power to the pedals. With this information it is easier to understand the importance that muscle power and aerodynamics play in increasing speed on the bicycle.

Sometimes, conceptual differences between strength and power are hard to grasp. **Strength** is the capacity that a muscle or muscle group has to exert force against a resistance at a *specified* speed. Once you are up to speed, strength will be used to maintain it.

**Power** is the time rate of doing work. It refers to force which is exerted explosively, as to bring about sudden acceleration.

In the annual weight-training program (periodization), exercises in the strength phase and those preceding it are performed at a steady, controlled pace, whereas the *speed* of exercises in the power lifts of the power phase is fast and explosive. Resistance training performed prior to the power phase of the program serves to systematically strengthen the muscles and connective tissues while increasing neural facilitation. In the strength phase, the repetitions per set are low, and the loads are moderate to high. This combination has been shown to produce the high motoneuron firing that is necessary preparation for explosive power cleans and plyometric exercises.

The power phase is the point at which training will become specific to the needs of explosive activity. Do not skip this phase, as it is very important to develop the ability to exert force against resistance at the speeds characteristic of cycling. Also, do not be tempted to skip ahead to the power phase without completing the progression through the previous phases, unless, of course, you are fond of ice packs and extended periods of rest. To be safe and to achieve the best results, take time to do the program correctly.

### How do I develop more power?

To develop more power in your body, you must perform explosive exercises. This type of training stimulates adaptations in the body that will enable you to respond with strength more quickly when you need it. **Power cleans** and **plyometrics** are exercises that approach the development of power in different ways. The power clean increases power output of the muscles by directly simulating a sudden acceleration against resistance. Plyometric exercises pre-stretch the muscle prior to contraction to bring about a physiological response that increases the speed at which the muscle(s) can apply maximum force. Each of these training techniques is very effective in developing muscle power, with the greatest results coming from a combination of the two.

### THE POWER CLEAN

This exercise is the most complex of all of the exercises described in this book. For this reason, we will carefully break down each phase of the lift into individual components. Novice lifters and juniors should skip this exercise during the first year of weight training. If possible, have a qualified

110

trainer teach you the proper technique of the power clean. If you are on your own, then visualize and practice each phase without a barbell at first. Once you feel comfortable with each individual lift phase, perform the entire lift using a broomstick or unloaded bar.

The power clean is an Olympic-style lift. Scientific studies have shown that Olympic lifts produce the highest power output of any human movement measured to date. Because this lift is so explosive when performed correctly, less resistance is required than on the slower, core lifts. Power cleans should only be performed after you have been lifting for at least three months. We recommend adding them to your program during the power phase (which in an annual January-December program would be in March), when your goal is to get to top fitness for the upcoming racing season.

## PREPARATION

On the days when you will be performing the power clean in your training program, there is a slightly different warm-up and preparation to insure safety and optimal results. As always, the warm-up will begin with at least 10 minutes of light aerobic activity. Before performing static stretches, perform some slow, controlled, dynamic stretches including neck flexion, shoulder rotations, trunk twists, hip rotations, knee rotations and ankle flexion. Additionally, prior to beginning power cleans, you should perform light abdominal and lower back exercises. To insure the best results and safety, this preparation progression is very important, and must be strictly adhered to.

## BEGINNING POSITION

- Assume a shoulder-width stance, knees inside arms.
- Position feet flat on the floor.
- Grasp bar with a closed, pronated grip.
- Grip should be slightly wider than shoulder width.
- Squat next to the bar, heels on the floor.
- Fully extend arms.
- Point elbows out to sides.
- Position bar over the balls of feet; bar should be close to shins.
- Position shoulders over, or slightly ahead of the bar.

[ BEGINNING POSITION ]

- Establish a flat back posture by:
  - pulling shoulder blades toward each other
  - holding chest up and out
  - and tilting head slightly up
- Focus eyes ahead or slightly above horizontal
- Keep torso tensed

## UPWARD MOVEMENT PHASE: FIRST PULL

- Begin pull by extending the knees
- Move the hips forward and raise shoulders at the same rate
- Keep the angle of the back constant
- Lift bar straight up
- Keep bar close to the body, heels on the floor
- Keep elbows fully extended
- Keep shoulders back and above, or slightly in front of bar

- Keep head facing forward
- Maintain torso position

## UPWARD MOVEMENT PHASE: TRANSITION (SCOOP)

- Thrust hips forward and continue pulling until knees are under bar
- Keep feet flat
- Torso should be nearly vertical and erect
- Keep shoulders positioned directly over the bar
- Keep elbows fully extended

## UPWARD MOVEMENT PHASE: SECOND PULL

- Brush bar against the middle or top of thighs
- Keep torso erect and head facing straight or slightly up
- Keep elbows straight
- Move bar explosively by extending the hip, knee and ankle joints in a "jumping" action
- Keep shoulders over the bar as long as possible, and elbows out
- Keep bar close to body
- Once up on balls of feet, shrug the shoulders
- At maximum shoulder elevation, flex and pull with the arms
- Keep elbows high during pull; keep them over the wrists
- Pull bar as high as possible

[ MIDWAY THROUGH ]

## CATCH

• Rotate elbows around and under the bar

• Hyperextend the wrists as the elbows move under bar

• Point elbows forward or slightly up

• Rack the bar across the front of shoulders

• Keep torso erect

• Flex hips and knees to absorb the weight of the bar

[ CATCH PHASE ]

## DOWNWARD MOVEMENT PHASE

• Lower bar slowly and control to top of thighs
• Flex hips and knees as bar lands on thighs
• Squat down toward floor
• Keep heels on the floor
• Maintain erect torso position
• Keep bar close to shins
• Place bar on the floor

## BREATHING

• Inhale before the first pull of the first repetition
• Hold breath until the second pull
• Exhale through the sticking point (shrug) of the second pull
• Inhale during the downward movement phase of succeeding repetitions

*Note: Description of power clean taken from* Essentials of

Strength Training and Conditioning *(pp.392-393)* by *T. Baechle, 1994, Champaign, IL: Human Kinetics.*

## PLYOMETRICS

Plyometrics is a term used to describe explosive exercises that are designed to increase power. The definition of power is the ability to generate force quickly, or speed-strength. This mode of strength training, originally called "jump training" came from the training programs of Eastern Bloc countries during the 1970s. Athletes from those countries were performing very well in explosive-strength sports such as track and field, weight lifting and gymnastics. Soon, coaches in the United States began incorporating "plyometric" drills into their programs as well, experiencing similar results. Today, plyometric exercises and drills are used by coaches in most every sport that requires high power output.

## HOW IT WORKS

Plyometrics is defined as an exercise that enables a muscle to reach maximum strength in as short a time as possible. The exercises are designed to provide a concentric (shortening) contraction of the muscle immediately following an eccentric (lengthening) contraction.

***Example:*** When performing the Squat Depth Jump, the athlete will step off of a box measuring 12–42 inches high and land in a 90-degree squat position, explode up from the squat and land solidly back in a squat.

The force of gravity is utilized in this exercise to create potential, or stored, energy in the muscles. That energy is immediately released by jumping up, instantly, upon landing. Research has shown that concentric contractions are more powerful when they occur in a muscle that has been pre-stretched by an eccentric contraction. It appears as though two physiological factors contribute to this phenomenon:

• The elastic components of the muscle are able to store a certain amount of energy when stretched, much like a rubber band.

• The *stretch reflex* mechanism of the muscle is a reflex contraction that occurs in response to sensory receptors sensing rapid muscle stretching.

## So how does this relate to cycling?

You cannot change the response time of the stretch reflex very much with training, but what can be changed is the *strength* of the response. The result is that you will develop a greater ability to overcome the inertia of an external object, in this case the crank arms. This *response strength* increase will give more snap when you need to answer an attack, power a short climb or react to a sprint.

## Proceed with caution!

Plyometric exercises can be dangerous, particularly if performed incorrectly. Take the time to learn the proper form, and practice each exercise before increasing the difficulty and volume of your training. Junior level athletes should skip this form of training in their first year of resistance training. Prior to undertaking a plyometric program, you should be in good condition and regularly stretch to increase flexibility. Be sure to perform weight-training exercises for at least eight weeks before adding plyometrics to your program. Aim for late hypertrophy to early strength phase in the weight program. Do not perform more than two sessions a week, and do not exceed 100 jumps per workout.

*Note: Athletes who have suffered chronic patellar tendinitis—kneecap problems—or have anterior cruciate ligament (ACL) instability should use extreme caution, and possibly consider skipping this form of exercise.*

## WHAT TO WEAR

It is absolutely essential that you wear a very supportive and well-cushioned shoe. Most basketball and cross-training shoes are perfect for plyometric drills. Clothing should be unrestricting and not too hot.

## SPECIAL EQUIPMENT

For the five recommended exercises the only special equipment required are plyometric boxes. These are not usually available, so be resourceful in what you use. Be certain that whatever is used is very sturdy and strong, and will not slip on the floor surface. For the squat-depth jump, for instance, a sturdy, flat bench may work, provided the cushioning is very firm. For the push-off exercises you may use a step-up box or Reebok Step.

*Note: To reduce chance of injury, perform exercises on a spring-loaded aerobics floor or in a room with a firm mat flooring surface.*

The plyometric exercises recommended for cyclists center on developing both the knee and hip extensor muscle groups. The following drills, when performed correctly, will help to increase power and explosiveness on the bike. For more information on plyometrics, see Donald Chu's book, *Jumping Into Plyometrics*. Remember, always perform a good aerobic warm-up of at least 10 minutes and stretch before beginning these exercises.

### 1. Bounding

*Equipment: None*

This drill is like running with a greatly exaggerated stride. Begin by jogging, and then push off of your right foot, bending your left knee and driving it upward until your right thigh is parallel to the ground. Your right leg is extended and held back until your left foot hits the ground, then is driven through and upward to the forward bent position. A strong arm drive will help you to achieve long strides. Perform for 30 yards then recover. Repeat 5-10 times.

### 2. Single-Leg Hops

*Equipment: None*

This exercise is similar to bounding, expect you will be landing on the same leg that you take off with. Drive the opposite leg forward as you strive for both height and distance with each hop. Perform for 30 yards then switch legs, perform five times each leg.

### 3. Stadium Hops

*Equipment: Large steps or bleachers*

Place hands on hips or at back of neck. Stand in a quarter-squat with feet shoulder-width apart. Jump up to the next step and quickly continue up the stairs for 10-20 jumps. Repeat 5-10 times.

### 4. Single-Leg Push-off

*Equipment: A box 6-12 inches high*

Stand with one foot on the ground, and the other up on the box. Explode off of the foot on the box, driving your opposite knee and both arms upward as high as you can go, then land in the starting position. Repeat 5-10 times each leg.

### 5. Squat Depth Jump

*Equipment: A box 12-42 inches high*

Stand on the box with your toes close to the edge and knees bent. Step off of the box and land in a 90 degree squat, then quickly explode upwards landing once again in a squat position. If you have access to two boxes, you can make this more difficult by jumping up onto the second box after landing. Repeat 5-10 times.

# CHAPTER EIGHT

# Program
## Information

*People write and call and ask me to describe a general training
week, but they don't need my general training week,
they need their general training week. They need to figure
their ideal training situation."
—Ned Overend
U.S. professional cross-country mountain-bike racer*

[ NED OVEREND ]

If you are reading this book, then chances are very good that you are your own coach. In fact, most cyclists determine their own training programs. Some gain information from more experienced riders, some are in clubs and teams that have a coach to guide them as a group, and others just carry on with whatever information they can find.

Now that you are familiar with the principles of weight training and understand the exercises, we will show you how to use all of this information to establish a comprehensive weight-training program. Helping you design a program that makes sense, fits into your lifestyle, and improves your performance on the bike is the primary goal of this book.

## PERFORMANCE ANALYSIS OF CYCLING

Maximizing the results of strength training starts with the knowledge of exactly what muscle groups need to trained. For most sports, total body movement analysis is necessary to be able to select the most effective exercises, and cycling is no exception. Fortunately, you do not need to attempt to figure this out for yourself. Exercise scientists using video cameras and computers have analyzed the complex sport movements involved in cycling, looking at each individual joint action. Understanding the specific actions of each joint, researchers have been able to isolate the muscles involved in each part of the overall movement. From this, a selection has been made of appropriate weight-lifting exercises that work each muscle group.

## LOWER BODY MUSCLES

Cycling is often thought of as primarily a lower body sport. However, as all experienced cyclists know, riding a bike involves the whole body. Who hasn't felt their neck and lower back stiffen after a 100-mile ride, or the arms fatigue at the end of a long, steep climb. How about the upper body and grip strength required to hammer a technical off-road descent? It is more than just the legs that need to be strengthened in order to improve bike performance.

Looking at the lower body during the pedal stroke shows a complex interaction of all of the muscle groups. During the downward portion of the stroke, the hip and knee are both ex-

[ MUSCLES WORK THE CRANK ]

tending, while the ankle is in slight dorsiflexion—toes pointing upward—in the first 90 degrees. On the upstroke, the hip and knee are both flexing, and the toes may point slightly downward (dorsiflexion).* The major muscles in the lower body responsible for these motions include the gluteus maximus, biceps femoris, semitendinosus, semimembranosus, rectus femoris, vastus medialis, vastus lateralis, gastrocnemius and the anterior tibialis. These are the muscles that provide motion about the hips, knees and ankles. The multijoint exercises of the lower body, such as the squat, utilize all of the above muscles in motions similar to cycling.

**Note:** *The motion of the ankle is referred to as "ankling," and differs greatly among cyclists. The positions described in this text represent what has been shown through research as the most efficient patterns used.*

## FROM THE LEGS UP

Maintenance of an aerodynamic position, absorbing shock, and stabilizing against the handlebars for increased pedal force production are just a few of the important aspects of cycling that can be improved by incorporating upper body and trunk exercises into your program. Off-road and track riders need even more strength and power in their upper bodies than a pure road cyclist due to the nature of those events. In addition to increased demand for technical bike control, the upper body, especially the elbow joint, acts as a heavy duty shock absorber during off-road cycling. The type of muscle contraction felt by the triceps to absorb bumps is an eccentric contraction. This action is easily simulated with isotonic weight training exercises, and will prepare the rider for more comfortable and safe riding.

## TRUNK MUSCLES

All of the muscles of the trunk are working during the entire cycling motion. The spine must stay in a very forward flexed position during riding, especially with seated efforts. Even when you are involved in an all-out standing climb or vicious sprint, the spine stays in slight forward flexion. The spinal erectors of the lower back work very hard to hold the trunk up against gravity by contracting eccentrically to support the upper body throughout the activity. In the aerodynamic position, these same erectors must work in an even greater flexed position to bring stabilization to the cycling position.

On the front and sides of the trunk is a group of muscles of-

[   A STRONG TRUNK IS ESSENTIAL IN THE AERO POSITION   ]

ten overlooked by cyclists who train with weights. These abdominals serve very important functions during all aspects of cycling. Each of the abdominal muscles; rectus abdominus, internal and external obliques, and transverse abdominus, works together to play a very important role in cycling. By providing proper stabilization of the spine and pelvis, the abdominals help limit the loss of power generated from the lower body. In addition, strong abdominals reduce the risk of developing lower back injuries while helping to improve breathing.

## UPPER BODY MUSCLES

The upper body is used in several different ways in cycling. Obviously, a downhill mountain biker needs more upper body strength and stability than a pure road rider. Yet, when that roadie needs to get out of the saddle to power a climb or sprint, he or she will need to have good upper body strength as well. Every muscle from the large pectoralis of the chest, to the small forearm muscles, is utilized in order to generate more power on steep

[ DOWNHILL MOUNTAIN BIKER ]

climbs, during sprints, or to assist in a technical descent or tight steering situation.

There are too many muscles in the upper body to list here. The important thing is to choose a weight program that strengthens each individual muscle group. To repeat something stated earlier in the book, do not worry about adding extra bulk and slowing down. An appropriate program is designed to increase strength without bulk, and keeps the most attention focused on the lower body.

## WHAT ARE THE SPECIFIC NEEDS OF A CYCLIST?

In order to increase the chances of carryover to sport performance, an athlete's weight-training program must be as specific to the muscle actions of the particular sport as possible. To get the most out of weight training for cycling, the program needs to be designed to develop cycling muscles in sport specific patterns.

The main focus of a weight-training program should be the lower body muscle groups that create the force applied to the pedals. This area of the body, often labeled the "power zone," consists of the quadriceps, hamstrings, gluteals, lower back and abdominals, and is the fundamental source of strength and power in cycling. The majority of exercises performed in a program should develop muscular endurance, strength and power of this zone. Weight training for the upper body completes the overall strength program, leaving no weak muscle groups.

## WHAT EXERCISES ARE THE BEST FOR CYCLING?

The exercises listed in chapters 4 through 6 are a compilation that includes exercises for cyclists ranging from general to specific. The general exercises center on overall muscular development and are performed exclusively during the first month of the program when general conditioning is the goal. The general exercises serve as pre-conditioning for the more advanced lifts that are added later in the program as training becomes more specific.

When the weight-training program becomes very specific, the exercises in the program are few and very specialized to the needs of the cyclist. At this time, overall strength is maintained, but carries much less emphasis in the workout. For example, during the power phase prior to the start of the racing season, there are a total of five to nine exercises in a workout. These exercises are almost exclusively targeted at developing the power zone in an explosive manner. When the racing season begins, the weight program emphasis shifts back to the general for overall strength maintenance.

### DIFFERENT TRAINING METHODS AND ROUTINES

As you learned in Chapter 3, one of the important rules to follow in weight training is to make sure that you do not repeat the same routine for too long. If the exact routine is repeated over and over, you will reach a plateau, and the benefits of your routine will be dramatically diminished. In addition to periodization, there are many different ways to vary the order of the exercises that make up your program. Most weight-training protocols have their roots in bodybuilding, but may be adapted to meet the needs of a the cyclist. Below are some of the most popular protocols that mix up training variables to bring about different effects.

## LARGE TO SMALL

Generally, unless under special circumstances, you should always work from the larger muscle groups to the smaller ones. The reason is that if you are trying to optimize the fatigue in each muscle group during a workout, and you do not want smaller muscle-group fatigue to be the limiting factor when performing more complex exercises. In the program, if you perform triceps extensions before chest presses for example; when you perform chest presses, the triceps, which are worked from the extensions, will fatigue before the larger, stronger chest muscles, lessening your development. When using the large to small muscle-group training technique, you will most often begin a program with legs, and finish with arms.

## SPLIT WORK-OUT ROUTINE

This training protocol basically refers to a program that trains particular muscle groups on specific days rather than training all of them during each workout session. This method is very popular in all phases of the cyclist's training program other than the transition and maintenance phases. The main adaptation made for the cyclist however, is that the muscle groups of the "power zone" will be worked every session, with the other groups split up between sessions.

WEIGHT TRAINING FOR CYCLISTS

## LOWER BODY—UPPER BODY

A popular routine used by many lifters is alternating a lower body exercise with an upper body exercise. When cyclists lift, they tend to overemphasize the lower body and neglect the upper. Most bodybuilders do the exact opposite. This method helps maintain a balance in strength development, and is useful when time is limited because there does not need to be a long rest interval between exercises.

## PUSH-PULL

Push-pull is a system of lifting similar to the upper-lower method. In this routine, choose an exercise involving a pushing motion (joint extension), and alternate it with one requiring a pulling motion (joint flexion). The push-pull method is performed by alternating following the completion of all of the sets of each exercise. This technique allows for greater recovery of muscle groups when they must perform more than one exercise in a workout.

## PRIORITY SYSTEM

The priority system states that the primary focus of the weight-training work-out should be to incorporate the specific exercises that the sport demands. Cycling, as stated earlier, focuses primarily on the "power zone" of the body. Therefore, concentrating on the legs and trunk when time is tight makes the most sense for a cyclist. One thing to note is that if your primary focus in cycling is mountain biking, you must not skip the upper body work in your routine as off-road riding places a greater demand on the upper body musculature.

## CIRCUIT TRAINING

There are many different types of circuit training. Since you will be getting more than enough cardiovascular conditioning on the bike and by cross-training, we will limit the discussion to circuit *weight* training. Circuit weight training can be a great addition to your routine, and because there is little rest between sets, it does not take much time. Circuits can be set up to focus on an individual's different fitness concerns. Areas such as specific muscular endurance, lactate tolerance, or maintenance of total body strength may be targeted in the circuit by manipulating specific training variables.

To help a cyclist develop a tolerance for operating at high lactic acid levels while maintaining muscular endurance, a special circuit program may be useful. Muscular endurance circuits that improve lactate tolerance are set up to incorporate about 12 exercises. Each exercise is performed for 45-60 seconds with short, 15-second rest intervals. The total workout consists of two to three circuits. The total body is exercised using a circuit that is performed three times per week.

Maintenance of overall body strength during the competitive season can be easily accomplished by completing two to three circuits of about 10 exercises. Each exercise is performed about 30 seconds and the complete work-out is done only two times per week. This time-efficient training can be performed early in the week so that it will not interfere with race preparation.

## SUPERSETS

This training technique serves as a great method for increasing intensity and adding variety while saving time. Supersetting involves doing two or more successive exercises for a given muscle group without rest in between. For example, do a set of shoulder presses and follow them immediately with a set of lateral raises. This forces a lot more blood into the shoulders and provides a very intense and effective training stimulus for the deltoid muscles.

A more popular method is to use the superset style of training for two different muscle groups that have an agonist-antagonist relationship with each other. In other words, on any given lift, one muscle is contracting and the other muscle is relaxing (such as the biceps and triceps when performing a biceps curl). For best results, choose muscle groups that are physically close together such as biceps and triceps, chest and back, or quadriceps and hamstrings.

## ASSISTED TRAINING

With "assisted training," which is sometimes called "forced reps," resistance is decreased in accordance with the muscle's momentary capacity to contract. With this technique, your training partner will be helping you to perform two or three post-fatigue repetitions, effectively lightening the load lifted. This method overloads the muscle(s), and can be very effective in bringing about strength gains.

By receiving a little assistance from your partner during the lifting movement once you are fatigued, you will be able to complete a few more repetitions, stimulating and fatiguing additional muscle fibers. Make sure that your partner does not help during the negative (lowering) part of the repetition. The eccentric contraction of the muscle during the lowering phase is essential to stimulating development.

A second form of negative training simply requires that you lift the exercise as you normally would through the positive phase, then lower the weight back to the original position as slowly as possible. For example, when doing the bench press, lower the weight as slowly as you can and do as many reps on your own as possible. When you get to the point where you cannot push the weight, have your partner help you to lift the bar, then continue to lower as slowly as possible. Because of the eccentric load on the muscle fibers using this method, expect to suffer a little more soreness than usual.

## BREAKDOWNS

Breakdown training works best with the use of machines. Choose a weight that you think will challenge you for a set of approximately six repetitions—50 pounds on the triceps pushdown, for example. Perform as many repetitions as possible at that weight. Once you have reached muscle fatigue, quickly decrease the weight to 30 pounds and, again, do as many reps as possible. This completes one set. Breakdown training enables you not only to increase the intensity, and thus force more blood into the muscle, but allows you to reach momentary muscle fatigue twice, affecting more muscle fibers.

This method is similar to breakdown training, except it is done with barbells or dumbbells. With this technique, you will quickly "strip" weights off of a barbell in 5- to 10-pound increments and continue the set for as many reps as possible. This may also be done using dumbbells working your way "down the rack" in the same manner. A set may include two or more weight changes.

## HOW MUCH WEIGHT SHOULD I LIFT?

K nowing exactly how much weight to lift each set can be very confusing. This question is the one we have been asked the most often by athletes beginning a weight program. Below there are three different techniques that are simple, and will help you to closely estimate the proper poundage for your lift.

### PERCENTAGE OF BODY WEIGHT

This method which utilizes a percentage of your body weight for both machine and free-weight exercises is a good one to choose if you are a beginner. This method is designed to give you a general idea of where to begin only. Additional resistance may be used on machines than with free weights, and resistances may be adjusted for different brands of machines. See the table below for approximate starting weights by body weight and exercise.

# Training Loads Based on Percentage of Body Weight

| Machines | % Body Weight | Free Weight | % Body Weight |
|---|---|---|---|
| 1. Leg Press | 30-50% | 1. Squat | 30-50% |
| 2. Shoulder Press | 20-30% | 2. Shoulder Press | 20-30% |
| 3. Leg Curl | 15-20% | 3. Dead Lift | 30-50% |
| 4. Back Extension | 20-30% | 4. Back Ext. Bench | 10-20% |
| 5. Ab Machine | 5-20% | 5. Ab Crunch | 0-10% |
| 6. Chest Press | 30-40% | 6. Bench Press | 30-40% |
| 7. Pec. Deck | 10-20% | 7. Dumbbell Fly | 5-15% |
| 8. Pulldown | 30-50% | 8. Bent Over Row | 20-40% |
| 9. Arm Curls | 15-30% | 9. Arm Curls | 15-30% |
| 10. Tricep Ext. | 15-30% | 10. DB Tricep Ext. | 15-30% |

Percentage of body weight method for selection of training loads for various exercise machines and free weight exercises. Adapted from Ward et. al., 1991.

# Percentage Chart

| 1RM | 40% | 45% | 50% | 55% | 60% | 65% | 70% | 75% | 80% | 85% | 90% | 95% |
|---|---|---|---|---|---|---|---|---|---|---|---|---|
| 30 | 10 | 10 | 15 | 15 | 20 | 20 | 20 | 20 | 25 | 25 | 30 | 30 |
| 40 | 20 | 25 | 25 | 30 | 30 | 35 | 35 | 40 | 40 | 45 | 45 | 45 |
| 50 | 20 | 20 | 25 | 25 | 25 | 30 | 30 | 40 | 40 | 45 | 45 | 50 |
| 60 | 25 | 30 | 30 | 35 | 35 | 40 | 40 | 45 | 50 | 55 | 55 | 60 |
| 70 | 30 | 35 | 35 | 40 | 40 | 50 | 50 | 55 | 55 | 60 | 60 | 65 |
| 80 | 30 | 40 | 45 | 50 | 50 | 55 | 60 | 65 | 70 | 70 | 75 | 75 |
| 90 | 35 | 40 | 45 | 50 | 55 | 60 | 65 | 65 | 75 | 80 | 80 | 85 |
| 100 | 40 | 45 | 50 | 55 | 60 | 65 | 70 | 75 | 80 | 85 | 90 | 95 |
| 110 | 45 | 50 | 55 | 60 | 65 | 70 | 75 | 85 | 90 | 95 | 100 | 105 |
| 120 | 50 | 55 | 60 | 65 | 70 | 80 | 85 | 90 | 95 | 100 | 110 | 115 |
| 130 | 55 | 60 | 65 | 70 | 80 | 85 | 90 | 100 | 105 | 110 | 115 | 125 |
| 140 | 55 | 65 | 70 | 75 | 85 | 90 | 100 | 105 | 110 | 120 | 125 | 135 |
| 150 | 60 | 70 | 75 | 85 | 90 | 100 | 105 | 115 | 120 | 130 | 135 | 145 |
| 160 | 65 | 75 | 80 | 90 | 95 | 105 | 110 | 120 | 130 | 135 | 145 | 150 |
| 170 | 70 | 80 | 85 | 95 | 100 | 110 | 120 | 125 | 135 | 145 | 155 | 160 |
| 180 | 70 | 80 | 90 | 100 | 110 | 115 | 125 | 135 | 145 | 155 | 160 | 170 |
| 190 | 75 | 85 | 90 | 105 | 115 | 125 | 135 | 145 | 150 | 160 | 170 | 180 |
| 200 | 80 | 90 | 100 | 110 | 120 | 130 | 140 | 150 | 160 | 170 | 180 | 190 |
| 210 | 85 | 100 | 105 | 115 | 125 | 135 | 145 | 155 | 170 | 180 | 190 | 190 |
| 220 | 90 | 100 | 110 | 120 | 130 | 145 | 155 | 165 | 175 | 185 | 200 | 210 |
| 230 | 95 | 105 | 115 | 125 | 140 | 150 | 160 | 175 | 185 | 195 | 205 | 220 |
| 240 | 95 | 110 | 120 | 130 | 145 | 155 | 170 | 180 | 190 | 205 | 215 | 230 |
| 250 | 100 | 115 | 125 | 140 | 150 | 165 | 175 | 190 | 200 | 215 | 225 | 240 |
| 260 | 105 | 120 | 130 | 145 | 155 | 170 | 180 | 195 | 210 | 220 | 235 | 245 |
| 270 | 110 | 125 | 135 | 150 | 160 | 175 | 190 | 200 | 215 | 230 | 245 | 255 |
| 280 | 110 | 125 | 140 | 155 | 170 | 180 | 195 | 210 | 225 | 240 | 250 | 265 |
| 290 | 115 | 130 | 145 | 160 | 175 | 190 | 205 | 220 | 230 | 245 | 260 | 275 |
| 300 | 120 | 135 | 150 | 165 | 180 | 195 | 210 | 225 | 240 | 255 | 270 | 285 |

## ONE REP MAXIMUM

Many work-out programs require you to lift a percentage of your maximum weight. It is important that you establish what that weight is as safely as possible. Once you have completed a couple months of consistent resistance training and are practiced at proper lifting technique, you are ready to determine your one rep maximum (1RM).

Utilization of the 1RM is the most common method to determine appropriate training load. Estimation of your 1RM is most often done on the multijoint exercises only. Core lifts such as squats, bench presses and pull-downs are generally the only ones tested. Accessory, trunk and small muscle group exercises do not require testing using this method.

In order to safely complete the 1RM protocol, you need to perform an overall body warm-up and then work your way up to the 1RM. Working up to a true 1RM should include about three warm-up sets of progressively increased weight and decreased number of reps. After taking an adequate rest of about two to three minutes, perform the maximum lift to get your true limit. One thing to note is that your 1RM will obviously increase over time so you must perform the test more than just once in a season. Try to retest at least every six to eight weeks, maybe even more often during the first few phases of your program.

## One Repetition Max Protocol

To maximize results from a strength training program, use of the one repetition maximum (1RM) protocol is recommended. To determine your 1RM, (which is maximum amount of weight that you can lift one time), choose a moderate amount of weight, and perform as many repetitions as possible of the selected exercise in perfect form. Once you have sacrificed proper form, stop, and note the weight and numbers of reps. Using the chart provided, determine your 1RM. Divide the weight lifted by the number corresponding to the reps. Follow the example below:

| | |
|---|---|
| 1 | 1.000 |
| 2 | .955 |
| 3 | .917 |
| 4 | .885 |
| 5 | .857 |
| 6 | .832 |
| 7 | .809 |
| 8 | .788 |
| 9 | .769 |
| 10 | .752 |
| 11 | .736 |
| 12 | .721 |

* Developed by John T. Allaire, C.S.C.S., Strength and Conditioning Coach, Clemson Univ.

**Example**:

You can bench press 150 lbs 10 times. Your predicted 1RM for bench press would be 150/.752 = 200 lbs

To be most accurate, perform the 1 RM test every 3-4 months during your training year to update your program.

## Training Outcomes at Various Percentages of 1 RM

| Intensity | Percent of 1RM | Number of Reps | Training Outcome |
|---|---|---|---|
| **VERY HEAVY** | 95-100% | 1-3 | Strength/Power |
| **HEAVY** | 90-95% | 3-6 | Strength/Power |
| **MODERATELY HEAVY** | 85-90% | 6-9 | Strength/Endurance |
| **MODERATE** | 80-85% | 9-12 | Hypertrophy |
| **MODERATELY LIGHT** | 75-80% | 12-16 | Endurance/Hypertrophy |
| **LIGHT** | 70-75% | 16-20 | Endurance |
| **VERY LIGHT** | 40-70% | > 20 | Endurance |

## REQUIRED REPETITIONS

The required repetition method is probably the easiest and most effective for many cyclists to use. This trial-and-error method requires you to perform the recommended number of repetitions listed in your program. After performing a warm-up set, the proper weight is determined by lifting a set of the assigned number of reps in the first set only, no more or less. For example, if your program says to perform four sets of five repetitions, you would want to choose a weight that can be lifted five times only. If the last repetition was easily completed, then you must increase the weight the next set. If you were unable to perform all of the reps, then lower the weight for the next set. The appropriate weight is one that you will barely be able to finish the last rep of the set.

## WEIGHT TRAINING FOR CHILDREN
## AND ADOLESCENTS

It is very important that parents and coaches are clear on the guidelines for junior athletes who use weight lifting to increase strength. Athletes under the age of 18, in particular, are at risk of injury because they are still in their growing years. Muscles, tendons, boney attachments, and even growth plates of long bones may be damaged from excessive force if juniors are allowed to use weights that are too heavy, or practice improper lifting techniques. The American Academy of Pediatrics has stated the benefits of short-term programs in increasing strength in young people without significant injury risk. However, the importance of supervision of youths by knowledgeable adults cannot be stressed enough in keeping the program safe.

In our experience of working with youths using weight training, the hardest thing has been to keep them from doing too much. Young athletes are competitive, and always ready to see "how much" they can lift. Limits must be placed on how much they are allowed to lift in each session and strictly adhered to. Below are guidelines that must be followed to guarantee safety and success:

- Undergo physical and medical check-ups before training
- Use strength training as only one of a variety of sport and fitness activities
- Use calisthenics initially to build muscle endurance and strength
- Use a variety of training methods: calisthenics, free weights, and machines
- Always develop proper technique first, with low resistance
- Include warm-up before training and flexibility exercises after training
- Progress from low resistance and high repetitions to higher resistance and fewer repetitions
- Exercise muscles through their full range of motion
- Restrict strength-training exercise to a maximum three times a week
- Use a circuit system approach to maximize cardiovascular fitness
- Avoid emphasis on negative or eccentric exercise (for example, lowering heavy weights)
- Provide constant and experienced adult supervision

## WEIGHT TRAINING FOR WOMEN

For all practical purposes, there is no difference between a general weight-training program for women than one designed for men. Since all resistance training programs should be designed to meet an individual's needs, it is unnecessary to differentiate between male or female. The only reason that we included this section in this chapter is because it is important to note the inherent strength differences that exist between the two sexes.

With regards to strength and power output, women average about two thirds of that of men. This difference is typically greater in the upper body. These differences exist because, inherently, men naturally have more muscle mass. In actuality, if you express strength per unit of muscle cross-sectional area, the force production potential is equal for both men and women of all ages. For this reason, it really is not necessary for men and women to follow different training protocols. If a difference is designed into a program for women, it should probably be to emphasize more upper body and trunk strength development.

[ A FEMALE RACER ]

# CHAPTER NINE

# Program Design

*"Train your weakness, and race your strength."*
*—Chris Carmichael*
*former U.S. road racer and U.S. national team coach*

D esigning a training program is never an easy undertaking. There are an incredible number of variables
that may need to be considered no matter what sport
you are training for. To simplify things, analyze what you
want. Ask yourself, "What am I training for?" Perhaps the
deeper question should be, why does anyone train?

Obviously, we all train because we want to improve. The
problem is that many, maybe even most cyclists know what
they want to improve upon, but few take the proper steps toward bringing about that change. If you want to become a better time trialist, just riding the club rides isn't going to cut it.
If you have special areas in which you want to improve, you
had better apply some specific training to those areas. Set
goals for yourself, and make plans to help you achieve them.

## GOAL SETTING

Overall improved performance is one of the main goals of all cyclists, but it is important to be more specific in goal setting. Think about what areas it is that you really wish to improve upon. Last year, did you get hammered on the climbs? Gapped in the breaks? Or dropped in the sprints? These are probably the three most common areas in which cyclists need to better themselves to be more competitive, all of which can be improved with strength training. Goal setting can force athletes to confront certain realities about their abilities and potential for improvement. By identifying our weaknesses and making improvements upon them, you will be able to remain focused and motivated in your training.

You may have noticed that the areas mentioned above center on improving specific cycling abilities and skills rather

[ A GROUP RIDE ]

than focusing on race results. The reason is that it is improving upon your weaknesses and increasing strength, endurance and power that will bring you good race results. It is important to set long-term goals such as winning a big race or upgrading a category. These long-term goals will help you plan your training and motivate you to stick with it. Just realize what steps it will take to get you there.

Putting goals on paper and continually keeping them in mind can nurture commitment and ambition. Write down what you want to accomplish in the upcoming season. Be sure to make short-term goals that will lead to those that are long term. These may be monthly, weekly or daily goals. This is what formulates an overall training plan on the bike, and what strength training will help you accomplish.

Goals are as vast as the number of individuals who make them. Your goal may be to compete in your first criterium, beat your Cat. III nemesis in a road race, or win the NORBA National Championship Series. Whatever it is, you must be willing to work on the areas that will make this possible.

> *"For me, it's like getting four root canals all at once:*
> *long, drawn-out agony."*
> *—Sue Fish*
> *mountain-bike downhill racer,*
> *who briefly considered cross-country racing*

Make certain that your goals are realistic. Do not make such a lofty goal that there is no way you can accomplish it. Goals like this may actually fall into the dream or fantasy category and are longer term than one year. Do not lose sight of goals such as these, but do not dwell on them to the point that it causes you disappointment when they are not achieved quickly.

Let's take the case of a Cat. IV whose goal is to make the national team. Perhaps a more realistic goal would be to upgrade to a Cat. III or Cat. II this season, then reevaluate his or her goals and plan for the next year. In this way, there are successes to be enjoyed along the way. Once you have experienced the satisfaction of "seeing" a goal accomplished, you will find it easier to set and visualize the accomplishment of future goals.

To be most beneficial, goals must be specific. It is helpful if there is an objective measurement of goals. Instead of simply stating "climb better," you may write a goal of taking five minutes off of a hilly time trial that you've done before. While you are in the weight room, visualize these goals and know that the training you are doing will help you to achieve them.

## PERIODIZATION

To get the maximum benefits from any exercise program, you need to have a good plan. Remember, most people don't plan to fail, they just fail to plan. You may or may not be familiar with the term *periodization*. If you have seen this word before, it was probably in a bicycle magazine or book presenting training program information. Periodization is a fancy word used to describe a systematic training plan. Basically, it is a process of structuring training periods over time to prepare for athletic events.

Credit for the invention of periodization should be given to the ancient Greek athletes who first used overload training plans to prepare for the Olympic Games more than 2000 years ago. The training plans were simple, consisting of using heavier weights and resistances over time to gain strength for competition. Further development of periodized training plans did not occur until early in the 20th century in Russia, Finland and other parts of Europe. Modern plans have been developed during the past four decades.

In the 1960s, a Russian physiologist named Leo Matveyev, along with Czechoslovakian sport scientist Tudor Bompa, developed a plan to manipulate different factors of training into a long-term plan of preparation for athletic events. The backbone of their plan was Hans Selye's General Adaptation Syndrome (GAS) theory that was introduced in the 1930s and explains an individual's ability to adapt to chronic stress. According to this theory, the body goes through three different phases when subjected to a training stimulus.

**1. SHOCK (ALARM).** During the first one to two weeks, the body's first response to training is negative, and is marked by muscle soreness, stiffness, and a brief decrease in performance.

**2. RESISTANCE.** During this time, the body adapts to the training stimulus by making physiological and mechanical adjustments that improve performance (also known as Supercompensation Phase).

**3. MALADAPTATION.** This phase characterizes the results of performing a program that does not change. Improvement has stabilized, and performance may drop due to overtraining, boredom or exhaustion.

With Selye's theory in mind, it is easy to understand the logic behind the designing of a training program that is varied and cyclic. A well-structured program will bring about the adaptations that occur during the first two stages while avoiding the negative effects of the third phase.

Bompa and Matveyev's work was further developed to emphasize phases of the preparatory period by American sports scientists Stone and O'Bryant. Today, periodization training programs are commonplace for athletes competing in all sports.

The long-term planning in a periodized program involves manipulating the volume, intensity and rest periods of the program to prevent overtraining and optimize peak performance. In an appropriately designed annual program, training will shift from activities that are high volume, low intensity and non sport-specific to sport-specific activities of low volume and high intensity prior to the most important races on the schedule.

The periodization program is a general plan for a cyclist's year-round weight-training program. The year is divided into three main seasons: pre-season, in-season and off-season. The seasons correspond to the cycling racing season of May through September. Each of the divisions contains different phases of training.

In the **off-season** (transition, strength and hypertrophy phases), you will work on getting a good base of strength before focusing on power and muscular endurance. The strengths you develop in the early phases of the program are maintained while new ones are developed. The **pre-season** (power and muscular endurance phases) gets the rider ready for upcoming racing by targeting cycling-specific energy systems. During the **in-season**, the goal is to maintain strength, and weight training is kept to a minimum as the rider concentrates on racing.

Periodization cycles are parts of the overall training period. The **macrocycle** is the largest amount of training time (a season or a year), but may stretch up to four years such as for Olympic preparation. Two or more **mesocycles** lasting several weeks to months occur within the macrocycle. These specialized blocks of training time emphasize preparation for key events and consist of a number of **microcycles.** The microcycle is the smallest portion of the training period consisting of the training days and sessions, and generally last about a week.

All of the cycles of a periodized training program are based upon preparation by increasing training stress appropriately to bring about an improved physiological response. The general model in most programs, most notably strength periodization programs, is the four-week "step load" program. During weeks one, two and three, the resistance load is gradually increased, peaking at the end of week three. The fourth week is a recovery week in which the loads are reduced. After the recovery week, the program may move to a higher level of weight loads, or to a different phase of training altogether. This model is important to understand, as it demonstrates the need to increase load to stimulate adaptation, while allowing for recovery periods along the way.

Setting up a yearly weight-training plan for a cyclist is easier to do than setting one up for on-the-bike training since the specialized preparation phases will all be completed prior to the serious races. An annual cycling plan must be designed to allow a peak for key events during the season, whereas the weight-training program serves only to first prepare, and then maintain strength for the cyclist throughout the season.

## What it all looks like

The following is a list of the different phases of a cyclist's periodized weight-training program:

**TRANSITION** (September-October) During this time, the emphasis is placed on recovering from the racing season and adjusting to weight training. This is a good time to do some off-of-the-bike activities and cross-training. Sleep in, stay away from club rides, and spend quality time with a significant other. You'll have lots of time to do other things since there are only two work-outs per week during this phase.

**HYPERTROPHY** (November-December) This is the time to start building muscle. Although the term hypertrophy refers to an enlargement in muscle fibers, do not worry about becoming the Incredible Hulk. Remember, this is not a bodybuilding program. You must, however, have muscle growth to increase strength. This phase centers on improving body composition (increased lean body mass-decreased fat), while addressing weak areas. You need to be dedicated to the plan, as you will be progressing to three, then to four work-outs per week.

**STRENGTH** (January-February) The base of your training is set, now you can begin to develop cycling-specific strength by utilizing multijoint exercises. To prepare for the explosive exercises in the next phase, the intensity and resistances are increased. During this phase, you will continue to work out three to four days per week. Paying close attention to rest intervals between workouts is very important now as the training volume is very high. Many of you (especially West Coast riders) will be increasing your bike work-outs during this time. It is very important that you do not combine hard riding days with hard lifting days. Do not let a meaningless February criterium wreck your program. Stay focused on the big picture!

**POWER** (March) This is it. This four-week phase is the key to your success! You should be feeling very strong now, and ready to do some explosive training. The number of days per week is now just three, and the number of exercises per session has been decreased. This change allows for the increased number of bike work-outs, while emphasizing quality over quantity in weight training. Work very hard during this intense phase, and you will develop the power to close gaps and win sprints.

*Note: It is suggested that junior level athletes should eliminate this phase or use great caution during this phase in their first year of weight training.*

**MUSCULAR ENDURANCE** (April) This is the last preparation phase, and it is designed to reflect the riding work-outs performed during the late pre-season (intervals and sprints). The weights are low and the reps are high, which means that the overall intensity is light. Do not skip this final phase, although early season excitement may tempt you to do so. This phase bridges strength training right into the season, and adjusts you to the maintenance phase.

**MAINTENANCE** (May-September) During the racing season, it is important to maintain as much strength as possible. Two training sessions are scheduled early in the week to allow enough taper before competitions. Prior to major competitions, taper a week or more, but do not quit your maintenance program. If racing a long season, it is very important to make time to maintain the overall body strength you gained in the off-season.

This program is general, and set up for cyclist's beginning their serious racing in May. If you plan to compete in early season races that you will consider important (races that you won't be training through), then the whole periodization plan should be moved up a month or so to accommodate that.

## OVERCOMING PLATEAUS IN YOUR TRAINING

*"A slump is like a freight train. You always know when one hits."*
*—Leonard Harvey Nitz*
*U.S. Olympic track racer*

Even with the variety that is a part of a periodized program, it is still possible to reach a sticking point in your training. If you find yourself feeling unmotivated because your training program has become stale, then you must do something to mix things up. In order to get past a plateau in training, try some of the following techniques.

*The following suggestions are for people who are not following a strictly designed weight program. Most complete programs already offer enough variety through periodization, and thus naturally include the following plateau-beating techniques.*

## CHANGE THE WAY THAT YOU PERFORM
### AN EXERCISE

The first way to get past a plateau and force further gains is to continue to perform an exercise, but using different equipment. For example, if you have been performing front shoulder raises using dumbbells, try using a barbell to perform the same exercise. Still another option would be to perform this exercise using the low pulley on a cable system.

In the case of the barbell bench press, dumbbells may be substituted, or a weight stack machine may used to work the chest muscles. These are some great ways to add variety to an exercise you enjoy doing while keeping your muscles "guessing," forcing them to continue making gains.

## TRY NEW EXERCISES

The human neuromuscular system adapts to specific movement patterns. This can work for you, but it can also work against you. Adaptation to movement patterns assures proper form in lifting patterns, which is a good thing. However, as was stated in part three of Selye's General Adaptation Syndrome Theory, if the training stimulus remains the same, improvement stabilizes and may even drop off. To prevent this from happening, it is advisable to change your training exercises occasionally.

For example, if progress comes to a halt in the bench press exercise, then either the incline bench press, flyes or dips can serve as excellent substitutes to "shock" your muscles and promote further progress. Although all of those exercises target the chest muscles, the different movements require different muscle-fiber recruitment patterns that will stimulate further strength and development.

## VARY EXERCISE ORDER

The way you organize your weight-lifting program should also be varied from time to time to keep you fresh. Try changing the order of exercises within a muscle group to bring some variety. For example, if in your chest routine you usually do the bench press first, then incline bench press, followed by dips or flyes, then try alternating the order; starting with the incline bench press, then do dips, followed by the bench press.

If you always do the bench press first, your upper chest muscles will never have the opportunity to be trained when they are fresh. Consequently, they will always be somewhat fatigued from being indirectly trained on the bench press. Simply changing the exercise order of each muscle group will add variety to your work-out and force new results.

## VARY THE NUMBER OF SETS PERFORMED

Another method to use when strength and muscle development reaches a plateau is to vary the number of sets performed for each exercise. If you have been training with multiple sets for each exercise, you may benefit from switching to a single- or two-set program for a few sessions. Conversely, if you have only been doing one set per exercise, you might want to try doing two or three sets for a work-out or two.

## VARY THE RESISTANCE-REPETITION RELATIONSHIP

Just as the neuromuscular system adapts to specific movement patterns, it also adapts to training work loads. Thus, another way to overcome training plateaus is to vary the resistance-repetition relationship. For example, if 12 reps with

140 pounds becomes a strength plateau, perhaps 8 reps with 160 pounds will stimulate further muscle development. If 10 repetitions with 80 pounds leaves you stale, then perhaps 12 repetitions with 70 pounds will do the trick for a while. The main objective is to avoid prolonged periods of training with the same amount of resistance and number of repetitions. Be sure to stay consistent with your training goals by not making too drastic of changes.

If you have reached a plateau in your training, and changes in your program do not seem to help, then you may just be overtrained. Remember way back in chapter three under the heading "proper rest, perfect results" we told you that you must provide proper rest intervals if you want to receive full benefit from your strength program. Well, we're going to cover this important subject in more depth so that it will be well understood and practiced throughout the year.

## RECOVERY

*"You've got to rest as hard as you train."*
*—Roger Young*
*U.S. track racer, 1973 U.S. national sprint champion*

The importance of sufficient recovery following a strenuous work-out cannot be emphasized enough. Most overtraining in athletes occurs when they do not allow enough rest time to bring about adequate recovery. This recovery time may be the rest interval between sets, exercises or training sessions.

The recovery process has been described by Michael Yessis as one which consists of three phases:

**1.** Ongoing recovery occurs during the course of the training session. Rest periods between sets or intervals allow the body to recover from each effort.

**2.** Quick recovery occurs at the end of the training session. Metabolic waste products are removed, glycogen and phosphagen repletion begins.

**3.** Deep recovery when physiological adaptation to training occurs. *See second phase of GAS theory.*

[ RESTING BEGINS ]

The recovery process can be enhanced by utilizing a number of different restoration methods either through activity or relaxation. We strongly recommend incorporating some or all of these methods into your training program. Each requires little or no effort, but can lead to a big difference in how you feel and perform throughout the year.

## DON'T SKIP THE COOL-DOWN

Most athletes understand the importance of warming up before a work-out, but relatively few make an effort to properly cool down after training. On the bike this may happen automatically as you spin home following a group ride, but after weight training, you will need to plan for a cool-down period. All it takes to enhance the recovery process is 10–15 minutes of low-intensity movement (stationary bike, a brisk walk) and light stretching. The benefits of a proper cool-down include decreased levels of blood lactate, muscle soreness and joint stiffness.

[ TAKE THE TIME TO COOL DOWN ]

## REPLACE THOSE BURNT CARBS

As we stated in chapter 2, there is about a 30-minute window of time in which it is far easier for the body to replenish depleted carbohydrate stores. Be sure to get a snack or energy drink soon after a hard workout, preferably one which includes some protein as well. Follow up with continued snacks or meals every two hours following vigorous training so that depleted levels of muscle glycogen can be replenished completely within 24 hours.

## FLUID REPLACEMENT

The importance of hydration has been previously stated in chapter 2, *The basics of weight training.* We can not impress upon you enough, how important it is to have good fluid intake before, during and after a workout. During winter indoor workouts, you may perspire more, and thus need to increase your fluid intake. Sports drinks such as Gatorade include electrolytes that may be lost during dehydration. Many athletes prefer to dilute these fluid replacement drinks if using them during training or competition.

## THE POWERS OF MASSAGE

Massage and cycling go hand-in-hand (at least at the professional level). The restorative capabilities of a good rub are well understood by athletes and coaches worldwide. When performed by a qualified professional, sports massage can help reduce muscle lactate levels by increasing circulation. In addition, muscle soreness and tightness from strenuous training may be relieved, allowing the athlete a quicker recovery. If you are unable to afford massage, self-massage techniques may be applied, and have also shown to be effective. Kneading and stroking of the muscles that you can reach yourself will benefit your recovery and alert you to areas of particular tightness.

## GET YOUR ZZZZ'S

*"Winning is a matter of training and tranquility."*
*—Alex Zülle*
*Swiss pro road racer*

Sleep can make or break an athlete during periods of hard training or competition. Maintaining regular sleeping patterns is an essential component to the training program. On days of double work-outs or exceptionally long sessions, a nap may be indicated to provide the appropriate amount of rest and recovery. Make your bedtime a priority and be aware that if you are not sleeping well, you may be overtrained.

# CHAPTER TEN

# Sample Program

This book has been dedicated to helping you to understand the world of weight training. The first few chapters of the book covered the important information on equipment and facilities that you will need to know. Chapters 4 through 7 then covered the specific exercises, and how to perform them correctly and safely. With this knowledge of the correct workings of the world of weight training, you are now prepared to go to the gym and not look like a "Fred" or a "Frieda."

The next step was to educate you on the systematic approach to designing an appropriate strength-training program. Once you understand the reasons behind the structuring of a periodized program, it is easier to use the basic model to form your own weight-lifting plan.

Below is an easy to follow year-round weight-training program for the cyclist. This program incorporates everything that has been covered in this book up to this point. The weekly workout plans for each phase are covered. They describe which specific exercises are to be performed, and at what resistance and intensity. Basically, we've done your homework for you. Now simply plug in the proper weights for each exercise and adjust the start date to fit your racing season schedule.

Hopefully, this book has been successful in its goal to help the cyclist to better understand weight training, and how it can help to improve cycling performance. Strength improvements come from consistency and dedication to your program, there are no shortcuts. Stick to the plan and thank us later. Good luck.

# ROAD PERIODIZED SCHEDULE

| DATES | NOV | DEC | JAN | FEB | MAR | APR | MAY | JUNE | JULY | AUG | SEPT | OCT |
|---|---|---|---|---|---|---|---|---|---|---|---|---|
| CYCLING PHASES | PREPARATORY | | | | | | COMPETITIVE | | | | | TRANSITION |
| WEIGHT LIFTING PHASES | HYPERTROPHY | | STRENGTH | | POWER | ENDURANCE | MAINTENANCE | | | | | TRANSITION |

# MOUNTAIN PERIODIZED SCHEDULE

| DATES | NOV | DEC | JAN | FEB | MAR | APR | MAY | JUNE | JULY | AUG | SEPT | OCT |
|---|---|---|---|---|---|---|---|---|---|---|---|---|
| CYCLING PHASES | PREPARATORY | | | | | | COMPETITIVE | | | | | TRANSITION |
| WEIGHT LIFTING PHASES | HYPERTROPHY | | STRENGTH | | POWER | ENDURANCE | MAINTENANCE | | | | | TRANSITION |

# TRACK PERIODIZED SCHEDULE

| DATES | NOV | DEC | JAN | FEB | MAR | APR | MAY | JUNE | JULY | AUG | SEPT | OCT |
|---|---|---|---|---|---|---|---|---|---|---|---|---|
| CYCLING PHASES | PREPARATORY | | | | | | COMPETITIVE | | | | | TRANSITION |
| WEIGHT LIFTING PHASES | HYPERTROPHY | | STRENGTH | | POWER | | MAINTENANCE | | | | | TRANSITION |

# JUNIOR PERIODIZED SCHEDULE

| DATES | NOV | DEC | JAN | FEB | MAR | APR | MAY | JUNE | JULY | AUG | SEPT | OCT |
|---|---|---|---|---|---|---|---|---|---|---|---|---|
| CYCLING PHASES | PREPARATORY | | | | | | COMPETITIVE | | | | | T R A N S I T I O N |
| WEIGHT LIFTING PHASES | ENDURANCE | | HYPERTROPHY | | | MAINTENANCE | | | | | | T R A N S I T I O N |

## BLANK PERIODIZED SCHEDULE

| DATES | NOV | DEC | JAN | FEB | MAR | APR | MAY | JUNE | JULY | AUG | SEPT | OCT |
|---|---|---|---|---|---|---|---|---|---|---|---|---|
| CYCLING PHASES | | | | | | | | | | | | |
| WEIGHT TRAINING PHASES | | | | | | | | | | | | |

WEIGHT TRAINING PHASE DATES:
TRANSITION -
HYPERTROPHY -
STRENGTH -
POWER -
ENDURANCE -
MAINTENANCE -

CYCLING PHASE DATES:
TRANSITION -
PREPARATORY -
COMPETITIVE -

160

# WORKOUT SHEET

WEEK#_____  WORKOUT:_____  PHASE_____  NAME:_____

| Exercise | RM | SET 1 | SET 2 | SET 3 | SET 4 |
|----------|----|----|----|----|----|
| 1._____ | ___ | ___x___ | ___x___ | ___x___ | ___x___ |
| 2._____ | ___ | ___x___ | ___x___ | ___x___ | ___x___ |
| 3._____ | ___ | ___x___ | ___x___ | ___x___ | ___x___ |
| 4._____ | ___ | ___x___ | ___x___ | ___x___ | ___x___ |
| 5._____ | ___ | ___x___ | ___x___ | ___x___ | ___x___ |
| 6._____ | ___ | ___x___ | ___x___ | ___x___ | ___x___ |
| 7._____ | ___ | ___x___ | ___x___ | ___x___ | ___x___ |
| 8._____ | ___ | ___x___ | ___x___ | ___x___ | ___x___ |
| 9._____ | ___ | ___x___ | ___x___ | ___x___ | ___x___ |
| 10._____ | ___ | ___x___ | ___x___ | ___x___ | ___x___ |
| 11._____ | ___ | ___x___ | ___x___ | ___x___ | ___x___ |
| 12._____ | ___ | ___x___ | ___x___ | ___x___ | ___x___ |
| 13._____ | ___ | ___x___ | ___x___ | ___x___ | ___x___ |

161

# TRANSITION PHASE

## WEEKS                                    1- 4

## GUIDELINES

- **Time of Year:** October

- **Intensity:** Minimum

- **Resistance:** 40-60% 1RM

- **Repetitions:** 12-15 per set

- **Sets per Exercise:** 1-2

- **Exercises Per Muscle Group:** 1-2

- **Rest Between Sets:** 1:1 work to rest ratio (30-60 seconds).

- **Workouts Per Week:** 2-3

- **Speed of Exercises:** Slow and controlled. Each repetition should last about 6 seconds, 2 seconds on the concentric motion, hold for 1 second on the contraction, 3 seconds on the eccentric motion.

### WORKOUT A  SCHEDULE

| Week# | Monday | Tuesday | Wednesday | Thursday | Friday | Saturday | Sunday |
|-------|--------|---------|-----------|----------|--------|----------|--------|
| 1. | A | | A | | | | |
| 2. | A | | A | | A | | |
| 3. | A | | A | | A | | |
| 4. | A | | A | | Retest | | |

# WORKOUT A

| Exercises | Week 1 | Week 2 | Week 3 | Week 4 |
|---|---|---|---|---|
| 1. Warm-up and Stretch | 10-15 Min. | 10-15 Min. | 10-15 Min. | 10-15 Min. |
| 2. Squats or Leg Presses | 40% 2x15 | 50% 2x15 | 60% 2x15 | 40% 2x15 |
| 3. Leg Curls | 40% 2x15 | 50% 2x15 | 60% 2x15 | 40% 2x15 |
| 4. Calf Raises | 40% 2x15 | 50% 2x15 | 60% 2x15 | 40% 2x15 |
| 5. Back Extensions | 2x12 | 2x15 | 2x20 | 2x15 |
| 6. Ab Circuit | 2x12 | 2x15 | 2x20 | 2x15 |
| 7. Prone Cobras | 2x12 | 2x15 | 2x20 | 2x15 |
| 8. Bench Presses | 40% 2x15 | 50% 2x15 | 60% 2x15 | 40% 2x15 |
| 9. One-Arm Rows | 40% 2x15 | 50% 2x15 | 60% 2x15 | 40% 2x15 |
| 10. Shoulder Presses | 40% 2x15 | 50% 2x15 | 60% 2x15 | 40% 2x15 |
| 11. Biceps Curls | 40% 2x15 | 50% 2x15 | 60% 2x15 | 40% 2x15 |
| 12. DB Triceps Extensions | 40% 2x15 | 50% 2x15 | 60% 2x15 | 40% 2x15 |
| 13. Cool Down/Stretch | 10-15 Min. | 10-15 Min. | 10-15 Min. | 10-15 Min. |
| Performed On | Monday Wednesday | Monday Wednesday Friday | Monday Wednesday Friday | Monday Wednesday |

# HYPERTROPHY PHASE

## WEEKS — 5 -12

## GUIDELINES

- **Time of Year:** November and December

- **Intensity:** Moderate

- **Resistance:** 60-75% 1RM

- **Repetitions:** 8-12 per set

- **Sets per Exercise:** 2-3

- **Exercises Per Muscle Group:** 1-2

- **Rest Between Sets:** 1:2 work to rest ratio (60-90 seconds).

- **Workouts Per Week:** 2-4

- **Speed of Exercises:** Slow and controlled.

### WORKOUTS B & C SCHEDULE

| Week # | Monday | Tuesday | Wednesday | Thursday | Friday | Saturday | Sunday |
|--------|--------|---------|-----------|----------|--------|----------|--------|
| 5. | B | | C | | | | |
| 6. | B | | C | | B | | |
| 7. | C | | B | | C | | |
| 8. | B | C | | | B | C | |
| 9. | C | B | | | C | B | |
| 10. | C | | B | | C | | |
| 11. | B | | C | | B | | |
| 12. | B | | C | | Retest | | |

# WORKOUT B

| Exercises | Week 5 | Week 6 | Week 7 | Week 8 |
|---|---|---|---|---|
| 1. Warm-up and Stretch | 10-15 Min. | 10-15 Min. | 10-15 Min. | 10-15 Min. |
| 2. Squats or Leg Presses | 60% 2x12 | 60% 1x12 70% 2x10 | 60% 1x12 75% 2x10 | 60% 2x12 75% 1x10 |
| 3. Deadlifts | 60% 2x12 | 60% 1x12 70% 2x10 | 60% 1x12 75% 2x10 | 60% 2x12 75% 1x10 |
| 4. Calf Raises | 60% 2x12 | 60% 1x12 70% 2x10 | 60% 1x12 75% 2x10 | 60% 2x12 75% 1x10 |
| 5. Back Extensions | 2x12 | 2x15 | 2x20 | 2x15 |
| 6. Ab Circuit | 2x12 | 2x15 | 2x20 | 2x15 |
| 7. Prone Cobras | 2x12 | 2x15 | 2x20 | 2x15 |
| 8. Bench Presses | 60% 1x12 70% 2x10 | 60% 1x12 70% 2x10 | 60% 1x12 75% 2x10 | 60% 2x12 75% 1x10 |
| 9. One- Arm Rows | 60% 1x12 70% 2x10 | 60% 1x12 70% 2x10 | 60% 1x12 75% 2x10 | 60% 2x12 75% 1x10 |
| 10. Shoulder Presses | 60% 1x12 70% 2x10 | 60% 1x12 70% 2x10 | 60% 1x12 75% 2x10 | 60% 2x12 75% 1x10 |
| 11. Cool Down/Stretch | 10-15 Min. | 10-15 Min. | 10-15 Min. | 10-15 Min. |
| Performed on | Monday | Monday Friday | Wednesday | Monday Thursday |
|  |  |  |  |  |

# WORKOUT C

| Exercises | Week 5 | Week 6 | Week 7 | Week 8 |
|---|---|---|---|---|
| 1. Warm-up and Stretch | 10-15 Min. | 10-15 Min. | 10-15 Min. | 10-15 Min. |
| 2. Lunges or Step-Ups | 60% 2x12 | 60% 1x12 70% 2x10 | 60% 1x12 75% 2x10 | 60% 2x12 75% 1x10 |
| 3. Hip Lifts | 2x15 | 3x12 | 3x15 | 3x10 |
| 4. Ab Circuit | 2x15 | 3x12 | 3x15 | 3x10 |
| 5. Incline Bench Presses | 60% 2x12 | 60% 1x12 70% 2x10 | 60% 1x12 75% 2x10 | 60% 2x12 75% 1x10 |
| 6. Lat. Pulldowns | 60% 2x12 | 60% 1x12 70% 2x10 | 60% 1x12 75% 2x10 | 60% 2x12 75% 1x10 |
| 7. Front Raises | 60% 2x12 | 60% 1x12 70% 2x10 | 60% 1x12 75% 2x10 | 60% 2x12 75% 1x10 |
| 8. Rear Raises | 60% 2x12 | 60% 1x12 70% 2x10 | 60% 1x12 75% 2x10 | 60% 2x12 75% 1x10 |
| 9. Triceps Extensions | 60% 2x12 | 60% 1x12 70% 2x10 | 60% 1x12 75% 2x10 | 60% 2x12 75% 1x10 |
| 10. Hammer Curls | 60% 2x12 | 60% 1x12 70% 2x10 | 60% 1x12 75% 2x10 | 60% 2x12 75% 1x10 |
| 11. Cool Down/Stretch | 10-15 Min. | 10-15 Min. | 10-15 Min. | 10-15 Min. |
| Performed on | Wednesday | Wednesday | Monday Friday | Monday Friday |
|  |  |  |  |  |

# WORKOUT B

| Exercises | Week 9 | Week 10 | Week 11 | Week 12 |
|---|---|---|---|---|
| 1. Warm-up and Stretch | 10-15 Min. | 10-15 Min. | 10-15 Min. | 10-15 Min. |
| 2. Squats or Leg Presses | 70% 2x12 75% 1x10 | 75% 3x8 | 60% 2x12 70% 1x10 | 60% 2x12 |
| 3. Deadlifts | 70% 2x12 75% 1x10 | 75% 3x8 | 60% 2x12 70% 1x10 | 60% 2x12 |
| 4. Calf Raises | 70% 2x12 75% 1x10 | 75% 3x8 | 60% 2x12 70% 1x10 | 60% 2x12 |
| 5. Back Extensions | 3x15 | 3x20 | 2x25 | 2x15 |
| 6. Ab Circuit | 3x15 | 3x20 | 2x25 | 2x15 |
| 7. Prone Cobras | 3x15 | 3x20 | 2x25 | 2x15 |
| 8. Bench Presses | 70% 2x12 75% 1x10 | 75% 3x8 | 60% 2x12 70% 1x10 | 60% 2x12 |
| 9. One- Arm Rows | 70% 2x12 75% 1x10 | 75% 3x8 | 60% 2x12 70% 1x10 | 60% 2x12 |
| 10. Shoulder Presses | 70% 2x12 75% 1x10 | 75% 3x8 | 60% 2x12 70% 1x10 | 60% 2x12 |
| 11. Cool Down/Stretch | 10-15 Min. | 10-15 Min. | 10-15 Min. | 10-15 Min. |
| Performed on | Tuesday Friday | Wednesday | Monday Friday | Monday |
|  |  |  |  |  |

# WORKOUT C

**Test**

| Exercises | Week 9 | Week 10 | Week 11 | Week 12 |
|---|---|---|---|---|
| 1. Warm-up and Stretch | 10-15 Min. | 10-15 Min. | 10-15 Min. | 10-15 Min. |
| 2. Lunges/Step-Ups | 70% 2x12 75% 1x10 | 75% 3x8 | 60% 2x12 70% 1x10 | 60% 2x12 |
| 3. Hip Lifts | 3x15 | 3x20 | 2x25 | 2x15 |
| 4. Ab Circuit | 3x15 | 3x20 | 2x25 | 2x15 |
| 5. Incline Bench Presses | 70% 2x12 75% 1x10 | 75% 3x8 | 60% 2x12 70% 1x10 | 60% 2x12 |
| 6. Lat. Pulldowns | 70% 2x12 75% 1x10 | 75% 3x8 | 60% 2x12 70% 1x10 | 60% 2x12 |
| 7. Front Raises | 70% 2x12 75% 1x10 | 75% 3x8 | 60% 2x12 70% 1x10 | 60% 2x12 |
| 8. Rear Raises | 70% 2x12 75% 1x10 | 75% 3x8 | 60% 2x12 70% 1x10 | 60% 2x12 |
| 9. Triceps Extensions | 70% 2x12 75% 1x10 | 75% 3x8 | 60% 2x12 70% 1x10 | 60% 2x12 |
| 10. Hammer Curls | 70% 2x12 75% 1x10 | 75% 3x8 | 60% 2x12 70% 1x10 | 60% 2x12 |
| 11. Cool Down/Stretch | 10-15 Min. | 10-15 Min. | 10-15 Min. | 10-15 Min. |
| Performed on | Monday Thursday | Monday Friday | Wednesday | Wednesday |
|  |  |  |  |  |

# STRENGTH PHASE

## WEEKS 13-20

## GUIDELINES

- **Time of Year:** January - Feburary

- **Intensity:** Hard

- **Resistance:** 75-85% 1RM

- **Repetitions:** 5-8 per set

- **Sets per Exercise:** 3-5

- **Exercises Per Muscle Group:** 1-2

- **Rest Between Sets:** 1:3 work to rest ratio (90 seconds).

- **Workouts Per Week:** 3-4

- **Speed of Exercises:** Slow and controlled.

### WORKOUTS E & F SCHEDULE

| Week # | Monday | Tuesday | Wednesday | Thursday | Friday | Saturday | Sunday |
|--------|--------|---------|-----------|----------|--------|----------|--------|
| 13. | E | | F | | | E | |
| 14. | F | | E | | | F | |
| 15. | E | | F | | | E | |
| 16. | F | E | | | F | E | |
| 17. | E | F | | | E | F | |
| 18. | F | | E | | | F | |
| 19. | E | | F | | | E | |
| 20. | F | | E | | Retest | | |

## WEEKS | 13-16

### WORKOUT E

| Exercises | Week 13 | Week 14 | Week 15 | Week 16 |
|---|---|---|---|---|
| 1. Warm-up and Stretch | 10-15 Min. | 10-15 Min. | 10-15 Min. | 10-15 Min. |
| 2. Ab Circuit | 3x20 | 3x30 | 3x35 | 3x25 |
| 3. DB Bench Presses | 75% 2x8 | 75% 1x8 80% 2x6 | 85% 3x5 | 75% 1x8 80% 2x6 |
| 4. Machine Rows | 75% 2x8 | 75% 1x8 80% 2x6 | 85% 3x5 | 75% 1x8 80% 2x6 |
| 5. Incline Bench Presses | 75% 2x8 | 75% 1x8 80% 2x6 | 85% 3x5 | 75% 1x8 80% 2x6 |
| 6. Lat. Pulldowns | 75% 2x8 | 75% 1x8 80% 2x6 | 85% 3x5 | 75% 1x8 80% 2x6 |
| 7. Rear Raises | 75% 2x8 | 75% 1x8 80% 2x6 | 85% 3x5 | 75% 1x8 80% 2x6 |
| 8. Shoulder Presses | 75% 2x8 | 75% 1x8 80% 2x6 | 85% 3x5 | 75% 1x8 80% 2x6 |
| 9. Hammer Curls | 75% 2x8 | 75% 1x8 80% 2x6 | 85% 3x5 | 75% 1x8 80% 2x6 |
| 10. Triceps Extensions | 75% 2x8 | 75% 1x8 80% 2x6 | 85% 3x5 | 75% 1x8 80% 2x6 |
| 11. Cool Down/Stretch | 10-15 Min. | 10-15 Min. | 10-15 Min. | 10-15 Min. |
| Performed on | Monday Friday | Wednesday | Monday Friday | Tuesday Friday |

## WORKOUT F

| Exercises | Week 13 | Week 14 | Week 15 | Week 16 |
|---|---|---|---|---|
| 1. Warm-up and Stretch | 10-15 Min. | 10-15 Min. | 10-15 Min. | 10-15 Min. |
| 2. Squats | 75% 2x8 | 75% 1x8 80% 2x6 | 85% 3x5 | 75% 1x8 80% 2x6 |
| 3. Deadlifts | 75% 2x8 | 75% 1x8 80% 2x6 | 85% 3x5 | 75% 1x8 80% 2x6 |
| 4. Single Leg Squats | 75% 2x8 | 75% 1x8 80% 2x6 | 85% 3x5 | 75% 1x8 80% 2x6 |
| 5. Leg Curls | 75% 2x8 | 75% 1x8 80% 2x6 | 85% 3x5 | 75% 1x8 80% 2x6 |
| 6. Calf Raises | 75% 2x8 | 75% 1x8 80% 2x6 | 85% 3x5 | 75% 1x8 80% 2x6 |
| 7. Hip Lifts | 3x20 | 3x30 | 3x35 | 3x25 |
| 8. Back Extensions | 3x20 | 3x30 | 3x35 | 3x25 |
| 9. Prone Cobras | 3x20 | 3x30 | 3x35 | 3x25 |
| 10. Cool Down/Stretch | 10-15 Min. | 10-15 Min. | 10-15 Min. | 10-15 Min. |
| Performed on | Wednesday | Monday Friday | Wednesday | Monday Thursday |
| | | | | |

# WORKOUT E

| Exercises | Week 17 | Week 18 | Week 19 | Week 20 |
|---|---|---|---|---|
| 1. Warm-up and Stretch | 10-15 Min. | 10-15 Min. | 10-15 Min. | 10-15 Min. |
| 2. Ab Circuit | 3x20 | 3x30 | 3x35 | 3x25 |
| 3. DB Bench Presses | 75% 2x8 | 75% 1x8 80% 2x6 | 85% 3x5 | 75% 1x8 80% 2x6 |
| 4. Machine Rows | 75% 2x8 | 75% 1x8 80% 2x6 | 85% 3x5 | 75% 1x8 80% 2x6 |
| 5. Incline Bench Presses | 75% 2x8 | 75% 1x8 80% 2x6 | 85% 3x5 | 75% 1x8 80% 2x6 |
| 6. Lat. Pulldowns | 75% 2x8 | 75% 1x8 80% 2x6 | 85% 3x5 | 75% 1x8 80% 2x6 |
| 7. Rear Raises | 75% 2x8 | 75% 1x8 80% 2x6 | 85% 3x5 | 75% 1x8 80% 2x6 |
| 8. Shoulder Presses | 75% 2x8 | 75% 1x8 80% 2x6 | 85% 3x5 | 75% 1x8 80% 2x6 |
| 9. Hammer Curls | 75% 2x8 | 75% 1x8 80% 2x6 | 85% 3x5 | 75% 1x8 80% 2x6 |
| 10. Triceps Extensions | 75% 2x8 | 75% 1x8 80% 2x6 | 85% 3x5 | 75% 1x8 80% 2x6 |
| 11. Cool Down/Stretch | 10-15 Min. | 10-15 Min. | 10-15 Min. | 10-15 Min. |
| Performed on | Monday Thursday | Wednesday | Monday Friday | Wednesday |

172

# WORKOUT F

| Exercises | Week 17 | Week 18 | Week 19 | Week 20 |
|---|---|---|---|---|
| 1. Warm-up and Stretch | 10-15 Min. | 10-15 Min. | 10-15 Min. | 10-15 Min. |
| 2. Squats | 75% 2x8 | 75% 1x8 80% 2x6 | 85% 3x5 | 75% 1x8 80% 2x6 |
| 3. Deadlifts | 75% 2x8 | 75% 1x8 80% 2x6 | 85% 3x5 | 75% 1x8 80% 2x6 |
| 4. Single Leg Squats | 75% 2x8 | 75% 1x8 80% 2x6 | 85% 3x5 | 75% 1x8 80% 2x6 |
| 5. Leg Curls | 75% 2x8 | 75% 1x8 80% 2x6 | 85% 3x5 | 75% 1x8 80% 2x6 |
| 6. Calf Raises | 75% 2x8 | 75% 1x8 80% 2x6 | 85% 3x5 | 75% 1x8 80% 2x6 |
| 7. Hip Lifts | 3x20 | 3x30 | 3x35 | 3x25 |
| 8. Back Extensions | 3x20 | 3x30 | 3x35 | 3x25 |
| 9. Prone Cobras | 3x20 | 3x30 | 3x35 | 3x25 |
| 10. Cool Down/Stretch | 10-15 Min. | 10-15 Min. | 10-15 Min. | 10-15 Min. |
| Performed on | Tuesday Friday | Monday Friday | Wednesday | Monday |
| | | | | |

# POWER PHASE

## WEEKS — 21-24

## GUIDELINES

- **Time of Year:** March

- **Intensity:** Hard

- **Resistance:** 70-90% 1RM

- **Repetitions:** 5-8 per set

- **Sets per Exercise:** 3-5

- **Exercises Per Muscle Group:** 1-2

- **Rest Between Sets:** 1:3 work to rest ratio (90-180 seconds seconds).

- **Workouts Per Week:** 2-3

- **Speed of Exercises:** Fast and explosive for the Power Cleans. Slow and controlled for all others.

### WORKOUTS G,H,I SCHEDULE

| Week # | Monday | Tuesday | Wednesday | Thursday | Friday | Saturday | Sunday |
|--------|--------|---------|-----------|----------|--------|----------|--------|
| 13. | G | | H | | | | |
| 14. | G | | H | | I | | |
| 15. | G | | H | | I | | |
| 16. | G | | H | | Retest | | |

# WORKOUT G

| Exercises | Week 21 | Week 22 | Week 23 | Week 24 |
|---|---|---|---|---|
| 1. Warm-up and Stretch | 10-15 Min. | 10-15 Min. | 10-15 Min. | 10-15 Min. |
| 2. Power Cleans | 75% 3x8 | 80% 1x8 85% 1x8 90% 1x5 | 80% 1x8 85% 1x8 90% 2x5 | 75% 3x8 |
| 3. DB Bench Presses | 75% 3x8 | 80% 1x8 85% 1x8 90% 1x5 | 80% 1x8 85% 1x8 90% 2x5 | 75% 3x8 |
| 4. Step-Ups | 75% 3x8 | 80% 1x8 85% 1x8 90% 1x5 | 80% 1x8 85% 1x8 90% 2x5 | 75% 3x8 |
| 5. Rear Raises | 75% 3x8 | 80% 1x8 85% 1x8 90% 1x5 | 80% 1x8 85% 1x8 90% 2x5 | 75% 3x8 |
| 6. Ab Circuit | 3x25 | 3x30 | 3x35 | 3x25 |
| 7. Cool Down/Stretch | 10-15 Min. | 10-15 Min. | 10-15 Min. | 10-15 Min. |
| Performed On | Monday | Monday | Monday | Monday |
| | | | | |
| | | | | |

# WORKOUT H

| Exercises | Week 21 | Week 22 | Week 23 | Week 24 |
|---|---|---|---|---|
| 1. Warm-up and Stretch | 10-15 Min. | 10-15 Min. | 10-15 Min. | 10-15 Min. |
| 2. Squats | 75% 3x8 | 80% 1x8<br>85% 1x8<br>90% 1x5 | 80% 1x8<br>85% 1x8<br>90% 2x5 | 75% 3x8 |
| 3. Deadlifts | 75% 3x8 | 80% 1x8<br>85% 1x8<br>90% 1x5 | 80% 1x8<br>85% 1x8<br>90% 2x5 | 75% 3x8 |
| 4. One Arm Rows | 75% 3x8 | 80% 1x8<br>85% 1x8<br>90% 1x5 | 80% 1x8<br>85% 1x8<br>90% 2x5 | 75% 3x8 |
| 5. Shoulder Presses | 75% 3x8 | 80% 1x8<br>85% 1x8<br>90% 1x5 | 80% 1x8<br>85% 1x8<br>90% 2x5 | 75% 3x8 |
| 6. Back Extensions | 3x25 | 3x30 | 3x35 | 3x25 |
| 7. Prone Cobras | 3x25 | 3x30 | 3x35 | 3x25 |
| 8. Cool Down/Stretch | 10-15 Min. | 10-15 Min. | 10-15 Min. | 10-15 Min. |
| Performed On | Wednesday | Wednesday | Wednesday | Wednesday |
|  |  |  |  |  |

## WORKOUT I

Test

| Exercises | Week 21 | Week 22 | Week 23 | Week 24 |
|---|---|---|---|---|
| 1. Warm-up and Stretch | 10-15 Min. | 10-15 Min. | 10-15 Min. | 10-15 Min. |
| 2. Leg Presses | 75% 3x8 | 80% 1x8<br>85% 1x8<br>90% 1x5 | 80% 1x8<br>85% 1x8<br>90% 2x5 | 75% 3x8 |
| 3. Deadlifts | 75% 3x8 | 80% 1x8<br>85% 1x8<br>90% 1x5 | 80% 1x8<br>85% 1x8<br>90% 2x5 | 75% 3x8 |
| 4. Lunges | 75% 3x8 | 80% 1x8<br>85% 1x8<br>90% 1x5 | 80% 1x8<br>85% 1x8<br>90% 2x5 | 75% 3x8 |
| 5. Leg Curls | 75% 3x8 | 80% 1x8<br>85% 1x8<br>90% 1x5 | 80% 1x8<br>85% 1x8<br>90% 2x5 | 75% 3x8 |
| 6. Calf Raises | 75% 3x8 | 80% 1x8<br>85% 1x8<br>90% 1x5 | 80% 1x8<br>85% 1x8<br>90% 2x5 | 75% 3x8 |
| 7. Hip Lifts | 10-15 Min. | 10-15 Min. | 10-15 Min. | 10-15 Min. |
| 8. Ab Circuit | 3x25 | 3x30 | 3x35 | 3x25 |
| 9. Cool Down/Stretch | 10-15 Min. | 10-15 Min. | 10-15 Min. | 10-15 Min. |
| Performed On | Friday | Friday | Friday | Friday |

## ENDURANCE PHASE

| WEEKS | 25-28 |
|-------|-------|

## GUIDELINES

- **Time of Year:** April

- **Intensity:** Light

- **Resistance:** 40-60% 1RM

- **Repetitions:** 15-40 per set

- **Sets per Exercise:** 1-2

- **Exercises Per Muscle Group:** 1-2

- **Rest Between Sets:** 1:1 work to rest ratio (30-60 seconds).

- **Workouts Per Week:** 3

- **Speed of Exercises:** Slow and controlled.

### WORKOUT J    SCHEDULE

| Week# | Monday | Tuesday | Wednesday | Thursday | Friday | Saturday | Sunday |
|-------|--------|---------|-----------|----------|--------|----------|--------|
| 25.   | J      |         | J         |          | J      |          |        |
| 26.   | J      |         | J         |          | J      |          |        |
| 27.   | J      |         | J         |          | J      |          |        |
| 28.   | J      |         | J         |          | J      |          |        |

# WORKOUT J

Test

| Exercises | Week 25 | Week 26 | Week 27 | Week 28 |
|---|---|---|---|---|
| 1. Warm-up and Stretch | 10-15 Min. | 10-15 Min. | 10-15 Min. | 10-15 Min. |
| 2. Squats or Leg Presses | 50% 3x15 | 45% 3x20 | 40% 3x25 | 50% 3x15 |
| 3. DB Bench Presses | 50% 3x15 | 45% 3x20 | 40% 3x25 | 50% 3x15 |
| 4. Back Extensions | 3x25 | 3x35 | 3x40 | 3x25 |
| 5. Step-Ups | 50% 3x15 | 45% 3x20 | 40% 3x25 | 50% 3x15 |
| 6. Machine Rows | 50% 3x15 | 45% 3x20 | 40% 3x25 | 50% 3x15 |
| 7. Prone Cobras | 3x25 | 3x35 | 3x40 | 3x25 |
| 8. Calf Raises | 50% 3x15 | 45% 3x20 | 40% 3x25 | 50% 3x15 |
| 9. Ab Circuit | 3x25 | 3x35 | 3x40 | 3x25 |
| 10. Biceps Curls/Pull-Ups | 50% 3x15 | 45% 3x20 | 40% 3x25 | 50% 3x15 |
| 11. DB Triceps Ext./Dips | 50% 3x15 | 45% 3x20 | 40% 3x25 | 50% 3x15 |
| 12. Cool Down/Stretch | 10-15 Min. | 10-15 Min. | 10-15 Min. | 10-15 Min. |
| Performed On | Monday Wednesday Friday | Monday Wednesday Friday | Monday Wednesday Friday | Monday Wednesday Friday |
| | | | | |

# MAINTENANCE PHASE

## WEEKS — 29-52

## GUIDELINES

- **Time of Year:** May-September

- **Intensity:** Moderate to Hard

- **Resistance:** 70-85% 1RM

- **Repetitions:** 8-12 per set

- **Sets per Exercise:** 1-3

- **Exercises Per Muscle Group:** 1-2

- **Rest Between Sets:** 1:2 work to rest ratio (60 - 90 seconds).

- **Workouts Per Week:** 2

- **Speed of Exercises:** Slow and controlled.

### WORKOUT K    SCHEDULE

| Week# | Monday | Tuesday | Wednesday | Thursday | Friday | Saturday | Sunday |
|-------|--------|---------|-----------|----------|--------|----------|--------|
| 29-34. | K | | K | | | | |
| 35-41. | K | | K | | | | |
| 42-47. | K | | K | | | | |
| 48-52 | K | | K | | | | |

# WORKOUT K

Test

| Exercises                    Weeks | 29-34 | 35-41 | 42-47 | 48-52 |
|------------------------------------|-------|-------|-------|-------|
| 1. Warm-up and Stretch | 10-15 Min. | 10-15 Min. | 10-15 Min. | 10-15 Min. |
| 2. Squats or Leg Presses | 70% 3x15 | 80% 3x10 | 85% 3x8 | 70% 3x12 |
| 3. DB Bench Presses | 70% 3x15 | 80% 3x10 | 85% 3x8 | 70% 3x12 |
| 4. One-Arm Rows | 70% 3x15 | 80% 3x10 | 85% 3x8 | 70% 3x12 |
| 5. Calf Raises | 70% 3x15 | 80% 3x10 | 85% 3x8 | 70% 3x12 |
| 6. Back Extensions | 70% 3x15 | 80% 3x10 | 85% 3x8 | 70% 3x12 |
| 7. Ab Circuit | 3x25 | 3x25 | 3x25 | 3x25 |
| 8. Shoulder Presses | 70% 3x15 | 80% 3x10 | 85% 3x8 | 70% 3x12 |
| 9. Hammer Curls | 70% 3x15 | 80% 3x10 | 85% 3x8 | 70% 3x12 |
| 10. DB Tricep Extensions | 70% 3x15 | 80% 3x10 | 85% 3x8 | 70% 3x12 |
| 11. Cool Down/Stretch | 10-15 Min. | 10-15 Min. | 10-15 Min. | 10-15 Min. |
| Performed On | Monday Wednesday | Monday Wednesday | Monday Wednesday | Monday Wednesday |

# REFERENCES

Anderson, O. "Things Your Mom Forgot to Tell You About the Periodization of Your Training." *Running Research.* August 1997.

Arnheim, D. and Prentice, W. *Principles of Athletic Training.* St. Louis, MO. Mosby Year Book. 1989.

Baechle, T. *Essentials of Strength Training and Conditioning.* Champaign, IL. Human Kinetics. 1994.

Blimkie, C.J.R. "Resistance Training During Preadolescence." *Issues and Controversies. Sports Medicine* 15 (6): 389–407, 1993.

Blimkie, C.J.R. "Benefits and Risks of Resistance Training in Children. In: Intensive Participation in Children's Sports." B.R. Cahill and A.J. Pearl(eds.). *American Orthopedic Society for Sports Medicine.* Human Kinetics, Champaign, IL, pp. 133–165, 1993.

Bompa, T. *Theory and Methodology of Training.* Dubuque, IA. Kendall/Hunt. 1983.

Burke, E. *Serious Cycling.* Champaign, IL. Human Kinetics. 1995.

Chu, D. *Explosive Power & Strength.* Champaign, IL. Human Kinetics. 1996.

Chu, D. *Jumping Into Plyometrics.* Champaign, IL. Leisure Press. 1992.

Clarkson, P. "Oh Those Aching Muscles: Causes and Conse-
quences of Delayed Onset Muscle Soreness." *ACSM's Health
& Fitness Journal.* 1(3): 12–17. 1997.

Faria, I.E. and P. Cavanage: 1978. *The Physiology and Biomechanics of Cycling.* New York, NY. John Wiley.

Friel, J. *The Cyclist's Training Bible.* Boulder, CO. Velo Press.
1996.

Gambetta, V. "Basic Considerations of Plyometric Training."
*Conditioning for Cycling.* 1(3):20–23. 1991–92.

Graham, J. "Power Strength Training Exercise Program for
Cycling."*Conditioning for Cycling.* 2(5):2–3.

Karvonen, J. "Importance of Warm-up and Cool-down on Exercise
Performance." *Medicine in Sports Training and Coaching.*
Dasel, Germany. Karger Publishers.

Karvonen, J. "Importance of Warm-up and Cool-down on Exercise
Performance." *Medicine in Sports Training and Coaching.*
Dasel, Germany. Karger Publishers.

MacDougall, J.D., Sale, D.G., Moroz, J.R., Elder, G.C.B., Sutton,
J. R., & Howard, H. (1979). "Mitochondrial volume density in
human skeletal muscle following heavy resistance training."
*Medicine and Science in Sports and Exercise* 11, 164–66.

McArdle, W.D., Katch, V.L., Katch, F.I., *Essentials of Exercise
Physiology.* Page 378. 1994.

Murray, R. "Drink More! Advice from a World Class Expert."
*ACSM's Heath & Fitness Journal.* 1(1): 19–23, 50. 1997.

Pearl, B. *Getting Stronger.* Bolinas, CA. Shelter Publications, Inc.
1986.

Radcliffe, J. "Training for Power: Part 1." *Conditioning for
Cycling.* 2(1):6–13. 1992.

Radcliffe, J. & Farentinos, R.. *Plyometrics: Explosive Power Training.* Champaign, IL. Human Kinetics. 1985.

Schlosberg, S, and Neporent, L. *Weight Training for Dummies.* Foster City, CA. IDG Books Worldwide. 1997.

Strauss, R. *Sports Medicine.* Philadelphia, PA. W.B. Saunders Co., 1984.

Strauss, R. *Sports Medicine.* Philadelphia, PA. Saunders. 1984.

Sleamaker, R. and Browning, R. *Serious Training for Endurance Athletes.* Champaign, IL. Human Kinetics. 1996.

Stone, M., and H. O'Bryant. *Weight Training: A Scientific Approach.* Minneapolis, MN. Burgess International. 1987.

Van Handel, P. "Planning a Comprehensive Training Program." *Conditioning for Cycling.* Winter 1991–92.

Walker, J. "This Season, Add Flexibility Training To Your Cycling Program." *Performance Conditioning for Cycling.* 1(7): 4–5.

Williams, M. "The Gospel Truth about Dietary Supplements." *ACSM'S Health & Fitness Journal.* 1(1): 24–29. 1997.

Yessis, M. Recovery. *Science Periodical on Research and Technology in Sport, 2.* July 1986.

# INDEX